MW01223033

Bulldogs & Bulldog Breeding

by

H. ST. JOHN COOPER

Vintage Dog Books
Home Farm
44 Evesham Road
Cookhill, Alcester
Warwickshire
B49 5LJ

www.vintagedogbooks.com

ISBN No. 1-905124-34-1

Published by Vintage Dog Books 2005
Vintage Dog books is an imprint of Read Books

British Library Cataloguing-in-Publication Data
A catalogue record for this book is available
from the British Library.

Vintage Dog Books
Home Farm
44 Evesham Road
Cookhill, Alcester
Warwickshire
B49 5LJ

"Everybody's Loved by Some One."

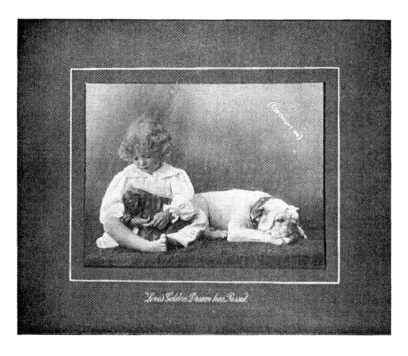

"Love's Golden Dream has Passed."

ECZOLINE ~~The Great~~ SKIN HEALER.

IT CURES Eczema, Rashes, Pimples, Spots, Ringworm, Sores, Chaps, Chilblains, Bad Legs, and Rough Skin, and will speedily remove all the terrible irritation, from whatever it cause will be at once allayed.

TESTIMONIALS.

Obtained from any Chemist, or from

HUNTER, REGENT STREET, SWINDON, WILTS., England,

At 1/1½, 2/9, 4/6. ECZOLINE TABLETS for cooling the blood, same price. ECZOLINE SOAP, 6d. per tablet. VETERINARY ECZOLINE made for the use of animals.

BULL-DOGS AND . . .
BULL-DOG BREEDING

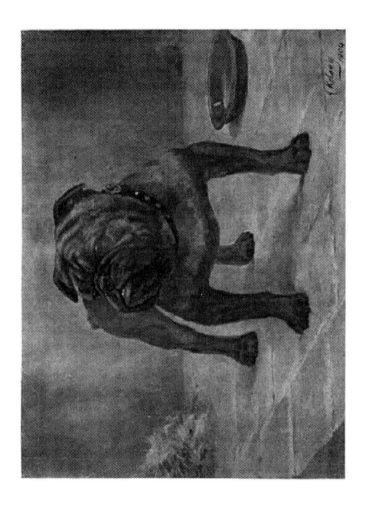

CHAMPION
"REGAL
STONE."

The property of

W. BUCKLER, ESQ.,
BROOKFIELD WEST HILL,
HIGHGATE, LONDON, N.

*From the painting by
Arthur Kelsey.*

Jarrold & Sons, Ltd., Printers and Engravers, Norwich.

BULL-DOGS AND BULL-DOG BREEDING

BY

H. St. JOHN COOPER

SANS PEUR ET
SANS REPROCHE

L & N

London:

JARROLD & SONS, 10 & 11, WARWICK LANE, E.C.

New York:

THE FIELD & FANCY PUBLISHING CO.,
5-7, DEY STREET.

CONTENTS.

CONTENTS.

LIST OF ILLUSTRATIONS.

INTRODUCTION.

To attempt to describe the origin and evolution of the Bulldog, and to give his history from his earliest days, is a task which the author at once candidly admits he is quite unable to perform. It is a task, moreover, that no man could take up with any possibility of certain success, for the earliest history of the Bulldog is shrouded in a mystery so deep and so complete that all efforts to bring it to light must prove abortive.

There are many who, practically ignorant on the subject of doggy lore, believe that the Bulldog has from time immemorial been an inhabitant of these islands. Their belief is mainly based on the fact that it is called the "British" Bulldog, and they have but little explanation other than this to offer. To these it must therefore come somewhat of a disappointment when they learn that the Bulldog of modern times is practically a manufactured breed of dog, evolved gradually from the nameless and breedless curs who far back in history made sport for their masters—who were themselves of the lowest possible type—by fighting, and by bull and bear-baiting. Gradually, as the sport increased in favour, these dogs were bred expressly for the purpose, and in the course of time became known as "Bulldogs."

Such is probably the origin of the breed, but it is practically certain that the Bulldog of to-day contains a considerable amount of Mastiff blood in him ; there is still so much similarity between him and the old English Mastiff as to give plausibility to the statement, though there are many who believe that the Bulldog is an offshoot of the less well-known Spanish Bulldog, of which breed some specimens were exhibited in this country some years ago by Mr. Adcock.

Be the truth what it may—and it is certain that the origin of the Bulldog is a considerable mystery—it is beyond doubt that as a distinct and separate breed of dog he was not known in England when Dame Berners, de Langley, and Dr. Caius made their contributions to Canine literature, for in the writings of

none of these is mention made of a breed of dog by name
" Bulldog."

That the Bulldog is an offshoot of Mastiff stock, and was in
the latter days of bull-baiting bred expressly for this sport, the
introduction of the Mastiff blood, giving him those qualities of
courage and determination which were so highly esteemed and
so necessary in a dog required for such a purpose, is probably the
solution of the puzzle. So gradually a strain of bull-baiting
dogs was built up, which presently exhibited marked characteristics, both mental and physical, which were fostered and
improved, and in latter days exaggerated by the breeders.

However, between the Bulldog of to-day and his ancestor of a
hundred years ago, there is, it must be confessed, a considerable
difference in appearance. The old type of Bulldog was that of
an extremely powerful and active animal, far more active than it
would be possible for the present-day low-to-ground specimen to
be. In fact according to modern ideas, the old type of Bulldog
might be termed a "leggy" dog, and as such would find but
little favour with those present-day breeders who aim at producing
a dog shewing as little daylight under him as possible.

It must be confessed that the modern dog with his exaggerated
points would come off but poorly were he set to the same work
as that in which his forefather delighted, and it is for this reason
that many are inclined to deride the modern Bulldog, and draw
comparisons between him and his ancestor extremely unfavourable
to the modern dog.

But there is much to be said from both points of view.
The Bulldog of a hundred years ago was a sporting dog
pure and simple; appearance counted for little, and all that
was asked of him was that he should be active, determined,
courageous, and powerful. Nowadays the Bulldog is not a
sporting dog, for the simple reason that his field of sport no
longer exists, bull-baiting having been suppressed by Act of
Parliament in the early part of the nineteenth century. It would
be useless, therefore, to breed a dog possessing qualities that can
never be called into use ; in fact, it may be said that it is utterly
impossible to do so, for Nature would step in, and, as is well
known, she never endows an animal with qualities or sense of
which it can make no practical use. Thus, for instance, fish that
are found in subterranean streams where no light penetrates are
sightless. There is, however, a mean way between the two types
—the old-fashioned fighting type and the modern show dog, and
there are few who can conscientiously contradict the statement
that, taken as a whole, in courage, determination, and fortitude,

modern Bulldogs compare very favourably with their ancestors. They are less savage certainly, which is not to be deplored ; they are also certainly less active, but that is the work of the breeder, and of altered circumstances. Still, though less active compared with the old type of dog, there is no reason that he should be a cripple. Both in wind and limb he must be entirely and thoroughly sound, and if the necessity arises for him to assert himself, he must be physically able to do so. That he has changed physically, is the work of the breeder. Points first introduced and bred for, for special reasons have been accentuated almost to exaggeration. No longer required for the rough-and-tumble life of the pit or bull-ring, he has been allowed to live at his ease for generation after generation, possibly with no harder task to perform than to take a moderate walk at his master's heels ; and so gradually his abnormal activity departed, his savage instincts were curbed, and the modern Bulldog was evolved.

While candidly admitting that the modern dog is the inferior of his ancestor in activity, and possibly in strength, and while denying that he is one whit the inferior of the older dog in courage, the writer would point out that our present-day Bulldog is far better suited to our requirements than the dog of a hundred years ago would be. There are very few among us who have the facilities, even if we have the wish, to keep a number of noisy and quarrelsome animals, whose sole delight lies in barking and biting. The possession of such animals would mean a peck of trouble for their unfortunate owner. Irate farmers would require compensation for the destruction of their peaceful cows, mangled and mutilated horses would have to be paid for, noise-disliking neighbours appeased ; in short, the life of a owner of, say, a couple of Bulldogs of the genuine old English type, would scarcely have a dull moment in it, but he would also have to pay very dearly for his excitement.

Than the modern English Bulldog there is no more companionable animal alive, despite what his detractors say; he can walk as far and as fast as his master, and though slow to anger, he is yet capable of giving a very good account of himself if peace can no longer be maintained with honour. He is a peculiarly even-tempered dog, and because of this trait he makes an admirable companion and playmate for little children, as he will submit to almost any torture, and never mark his disapproval by so much as a growl.

The writer speaks, it must be clearly understood, of Bulldogs generally. There are exceptions, of course, bad-tempered Bulldogs as there are bad-tempered people, and they—the animals and the people—should be avoided when possible. There are also weedy, crippled specimens, scarcely capable of crawling, and which are fit for nothing but to lie in their kennels or on a rug before the fire all day. For such dogs as these the sensible man and woman will have no use. They are produced by injudicious breeding, and a bad system of feeding, persisted in from generation to generation by the ignorant. They are also produced by the cupidity of certain of the lower class of dog owner, who keep inferior stud dogs simply as money-making machines, and who make use of the animals until they are on their last legs, with the result that there is a possibility of the country being flooded with weedy, undersized, anæmic and generally unthrifty and undesirable puppies that are bought and sold for a matter of two or three pounds, and are in reality not worth as many pence.

The man who buys such puppies buys trouble, and his initial outlay is soon considerably augmented by veterinary surgeon's fees, medicines, patent foods, and the hundred-and-one things that he will feel compelled to purchase and thrust down the throat of the unhappy animal, until death releases it.

The man who buys a young puppy will do well not to trust entirely to specious advertisements. He should satisfy himself that the much-vaunted dog who is advertised as sire of the puppy, or the " grand "—a favourite word this with advertisers—bitch who is its dam, are not a couple of poor, unhealthy animals who have been badly fed and badly housed all their lives, and from whom a good strong and healthy puppy is an utter impossibility.

As has been before stated, the marked change in the appearance of the Bulldog of to-day compared with the dog of bull-baiting days, is due to the efforts of the breeder who has by careful selection accentuated certain desirable points and repressed others ; and as all breeders have not worked on exactly the same lines, the result is that there are several distinct types of modern Bulldogs, which all conform more or less to the dictates of the standard of the breed issued by the premier Bulldog club, the Bulldog Club Incorporated, but which are so distinct one from another that even the novice may distinguish between them. There is, for example, the type of dog that has been called by admirers of the old-fashioned fighting stock by the name, " Glorified Pugs," and which, it must be admitted, well deserves this uncomplimentary designation.

This dog is generally " soft " in appearance, and totally lacking that characteristic sour expression which is a proper and very necessary Bulldog attribute. He is, in fact, far more like an overgrown pug than a Bulldog, and "pugginess" is abominable

An old English Bull-
dog of 80 years
ago.

Drawn and Engraved by Thomas Landseer. LITTLE BILLY. A Celebrated Bull Dog.

Pub'd by Sherwood & C° Dec 1, 182...

Reproduced by per-
mission of " The
Illustrated Kennel
News."

in the sight of all true Bulldog men. When this stamp of dog is of an apricot or fawn colour, with a black mask to his face, the likeness to the pug is accentuated, and it is hard sometimes to believe that the animal has any claim to the name Bulldog at all. But in order that the novice should not be permitted at the outset to fall into error, it should be stated here that while a "puggy" Bulldog may often be, and very often is, of a fawn or red colour, it does not follow that every fawn-coloured dog is puggy. There are many exceptionally good fawn or red Bull-dogs, which have taken deservedly high honours at leading shows, and fawn or red is, according to the Bulldog Club standards, a permissible and even desirable colour, though there are many old-fashioned breeders, and, for the matter of that, breeders who cannot claim to be old-fashioned, who have no particular love for the colour, and greatly prefer to see their dogs white, brindle, or white marked with brindle patches ; and of these colours the last, which is usually called brindle-pied, is the most characteristic.

Then we have another type of dog, and the one which all breeders should aim at reproducing—the sturdy, fierce-looking dog, with capacious jaw, massive skull and bone, and that air of determination, and even ferocity, which makes him look a formidable opponent, and the sight of which is enough to scare away tramps, housebreakers, and similar gentry.

It does not, however, follow that the dog's nature is in harmony with his appearance. He looks formidable, as he indeed is if his angry passions are aroused, but those passions are not easily aroused, and in the ordinary way he is as mild and gentle as the proverbial lamb, and eminently trustworthy with humankind, big and small, and animals of his own species.

It cannot be too frequently impressed that a Bulldog should look like a Bulldog and like nothing else. It is not sufficient that a dog answers to the description laid down by the standard ; it is not sufficient that he is big-boned, low on the forelegs, big skulled, short in back, perfect in ear and tail-carriage, and so on. If he lacks character and expression he is marred ! He is not a true Bulldog if he has a soft and benign expression of countenance ; he is not a true Bulldog if he betrays any weak-ness of character. Physically and mentally he must be strong, as the Bulldog Club standard puts it ; he must convey an impression of determination, strength, and activity similar to that suggested by the appearance of a thick-set Ayrshire or Highland bull. It is scarcely necessary to add more to this.

There are many queer notions prevalent among the ignorant

concerning Bulldogs, and it has been the lot of the writer to receive many letters which betray an amount of ignorance of the Bulldog on the part of the writers that is simply colossal. One very prevalent idea is that the forelegs of the Bulldog should be bowed, or bandy ; in fact, several would-be purchasers of Bulldogs have insisted on this, to their idea, necessary point, which is, in reality, highly detrimental.

A Bulldog's legs must be straight; the forelegs are wide apart, but the distance from leg to leg is not due to a bent bone, but to the width and massiveness of the chest. On this subject more will be said in the chapter in which the build and formation of the dog is dealt with.

Another queer and erroneous notion is that the tail of a Bulldog should be broken during puppyhood. This idea is due to the fact that many Bulldogs possess what is termed a crank tail. It is a point that is highly esteemed by many, but which is in reality by no means necessary. There is, however, some excuse for those who have acquired this notion, as there is a strong resemblance between a crank tail and a tail which, originally straight, has been broken and badly set, or not set at all.

The question that every man should ask himself before he enters the ranks of Bulldog fanciers is, Is he sufficiently interested in the breed to put up with many and many a disappointment, to face a certain amount of financial loss, and to devote such time as he can give to the welfare of his dog? If he can answer this in the affirmative, then there is room for him. If, on the other hand, his idea in taking up Bulldogs is that he anticipates making money by them, then let him at once dismiss the idea and the thought of becoming a Bulldog breeder. The writer does not, however, wish to convey the idea that every man who sets about breeding Bulldogs must meet with nothing but disappointment and loss ; that would be as absurd as stating that breeding Bulldogs is an easy and simple means of amassing a fortune.

The beginner will have much to learn and many difficulties to overcome, but there is no reason, if he possesses a good stock of patience and a genuine love for the dog, why in the course of time he should not achieve some meed of success. It is not every man who can breed a champion from his first litter, and he who starts with that idea in view will assuredly be disappointed. It is, however, a healthy ambition to look forward to breed a champion dog one day, and the man who sets to work with that end in view, and who has something of the Bulldog pertinacity and tenacity in his own composition, who is patient under defeat and disappointment, who is not above learning from those who have every reason for knowing better than himself, and who does not over-rate his own ability and his own stock, may, and very likely will, succeed—in time.

H. ST. JOHN COOPER.

Brighton, 1905.

BULLDOGS

AND

BULLDOG BREEDING.

CHAPTER I.

BUYING A BULLDOG—THE MARKET VALUE OF BULLDOGS—SALE
AND EXCHANGE ADVERTISEMENTS—PROTECTION FROM FRAUD
—THE CANINE PRESS.

NATURALLY the first thought of the embryo Bulldog man will
be the acquisition of a dog, and as his initial venture in this
direction will in all probability have a marked effect on his
subsequent career as a Bulldog fancier, he will do well to
consider deeply before taking the all-important step.

In the first place he will be obliged to make his purchase
according to his means, and if his means are not considerable
his choice will in consequence be somewhat restricted ; while,
on the other hand, when money is a secondary consideration, he
will have a far greater selection, but must be well on his guard,
or he may become the prey of the unscrupulous.

The first thing that he must decide is for what purpose does
he require a dog. Does he wish to at once blossom out as an
exhibitor, or does he propose to go in seriously for breeding, or
does he require a dog merely for companionship?

It may be accepted that these are the three primary reasons
that are responsible for the purchase of a dog.

If he requires a dog for exhibition, he must be prepared
to pay a good price for him, and if he is not prepared to pay a
respectable amount he must give up all thought of purchasing a
mature dog, and must select a young puppy, trusting to fortune
that he will rear it, and that it will develop into a good dog.
The man who is prepared to pay for his requirements should

attend some of the larger shows, where he will gain a considerable amount of knowledge by careful examination of the various
dogs exhibited, and by comparing those who have won prizes
with those who have not. Yet he must not pin his faith too
entirely on the judges' placings of the dogs, for it is a fact that
a dog may do a considerable amount of winning at one show
under a certain judge, while possibly in the same week he may,
at another show and under another judge, receive scarcely any
attention at all. And it does not follow in every case that one of
the judges is incompetent. Judges, like ordinary men, are but
human, and have their fads and fancies, and while a dog may
strike one man very favourably, another man may see a host of
faults in the same animal to which the first was either blind or
very lenient.

The man who is on the look-out for a prize-winning dog should
therefore attend not one show, but many, and should be in no
desperate hurry to make his purchase. If a dog is consistently
put into a high position by various judges, then he may safely
assume that the animal is a good one, and that he cannot be
doing very wrongly if he purchases him at a reasonable figure.

And what is a reasonable figure? one would naturally ask,
and it is a question that is exceedingly difficult to answer.   .

A really first-class Bulldog may be valued at anything from
one hundred pounds to a thousand, at which latter price several
have been sold ; and, as a matter of fact, very few really good
dogs can be bought at the lesser figure, the average price for a
good Bulldog, a winner of many prizes, being anything from one
to five hundred pounds ; and if a buyer can buy a really good
animal for anything less than a hundred pounds he is fortunate,
and may congratulate himself on having secured a bargain.

But the fact that these big prices rule need not deter the
man of small means, nor dishearten him. There are many
first-rate puppies that have changed hands during the earlier
stage of their existence for from ten to twenty pounds, and
have developed into dogs for which ten times the original sum
might be fairly asked and easily obtained.   .

Thus it will be seen that the man who determines to buy a
dog for exhibition must be controlled entirely by the condition
of his purse. Pleasant though it may be to be able to afford
to indulge one's tastes regardless of cost, there is more real
satisfaction, from a sporting view, to be obtained from the
successes of a dog that has either been bred by the exhibitor,
or purchased by him at a very early age. Anyone, providing
he is sufficiently wealthy, may purchase a winning dog, but it is

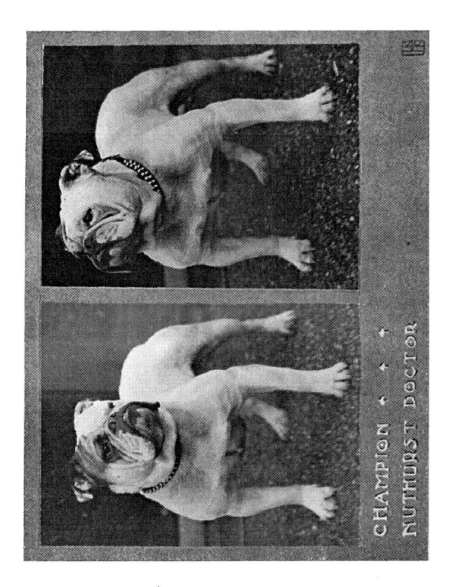

CHAMPION + + +
NUTHURST DOCTOR.

CHAMPION
"NUTHURST
DOCTOR."

The property of

MRS. EDGAR WATERLOW,

64, COMPAYNE GARDENS,

W. HAMPSTEAD, LONDON.

Photo by
H. St. John Cooper,
Brighton.

not everyone who is able to win with home-bred ones, and the beginner who is anxious to shine in the show ring will do well to curb his impatience, and instead of immediately blossoming forth as the owner of a full-fledged champion, he should rather lay out his money in the purchase of one or two really high-class brood bitches, and, possibly, a good stud dog,'and set to work to produce his own winners. That he may not at first succeed is very probable, but when success does come, as it usually will, eventually, to the persistent, it will be appreciated all the more.

The man with plenty of money at his disposal, who is wishing to start a Bulldog kennel, would do well to buy one or two young and healthy brood bitches of good breeding, a dog that has made his mark at stud and has sired winners, though himself possibly not a show specimen, as is often enough the case, and in addition to these, one or two really good and promising youngsters of both sexes, and of ages varying from three to six months.

The young brood bitches he will breed from as they come into use, and while these breeding operations are in progress, the young stock that he has bought will be developing into either show dogs or bitches, or into some more useful breeding stock.

But it is not everyone who is able to purchase on so generous a scale, and to the average man a matter of five to ten pounds outlay on the purchase of a dog is a consideration of some moment. Such buyers have three alternatives open to them: The purchase of a dog that is quite useless for showing, but which, as a companion, will prove very likely as good, and perhaps better, than any show dog; the purchase of a good though plain brood bitch; or the purchase of a young puppy from the nest.

If he decides on the first course, it is hardly necessary to say anything. He will buy any dog that takes his fancy, and will pay anything from a couple of pounds upwards.

The purchase of a brood bitch, however, requires a great deal more consideration and care. In the first place, she should be of undoubted pedigree, and not more than three years of age at the most; if younger so much the better. As to her points, they will be dealt with at some length in a later chapter. Above all, she must be healthy, and the purchaser must assure himself of this fact; and to make assurance doubly sure, he might, with advantage, submit her to a veterinary examination, and, in particular, tumorous growths, unfortunately too common to the breed, should be looked for, and, if found, the animal discarded as useless.

"CORSHAM BOGIE."

The property of
MRS. W. HUGH BERNERS,
INWARD, SUDBURY,
SUFFOLK.

There are very many ways of purchasing a dog. Some are bought through the medium of shows, but these are usually high-priced dogs, and by far the greater number of dogs change hands through the medium of the columns of *The Bazaar, Exchange, and Mart*, and the prepaid advertisement columns of the leading kennel journals, *Our Dogs, The Stock-keeper*, and the *Illustrated Kennel News*.

In any of these four papers are to be found, week by week, numerous advertisements, in which Bulldogs are offered for sale at all prices ranging from a couple of pounds to as many hundreds, and the difficulty that the novice will have will be to determine which of the many dogs offered is likely to suit his requirements, and who of the many advertisers are likely to treat him fairly and honourably.

It is satisfactory to be able to say that, taken as a whole, by far the greater proportion of dog owners who use the columns of these papers are straightforward and honourable men, but there are black sheep in every fold, and against these the novice, and, indeed, the older hand too, must be on his guard.

In order that he may effectively secure himself against the machinations of the dishonest, he should take advantage of the admirable deposit system that was inaugurated by *The Bazaar, Exchange, and Mart*, and which is in general use with most papers that publish private sale and exchange advertisements.

Briefly, the system is as follows : The buyer, having decided in favour of a certain dog, arranges with the owner that the dog shall be sent to him on approval. It is generally understood that the intending purchaser pays the carriage on the dog to and from in the event of the dog not being approved of. This arrangement having been made, the intending purchaser forwards a money order, postal orders, or bank notes to the editor of the paper in which the advertisement appears, to the value of the dog, plus a small percentage which is charged by the paper for its trouble and expense in the matter. On receipt of the deposit, the editor advises the seller of the dog, who thereon sends the animal according to arrangement. If the purchase is completed, the money is then sent on to the seller by the editor, and the matter is at an end. If the animal is not approved of, he is returned to the sender, and the buyer applies to the editor for the return of his deposit, less the small commission.

This is by far the better plan to pursue, but there is another method which is sometimes practised, but which is less satisfactory than the foregoing. A post-dated cheque is sent by the buyer, on receipt of which the dog is forwarded by the seller.

"JUSTICE OF PEACE."

The property of
MRS. W. HUGH BERNERS,
INWARD, SUDBURY, SUFFOLK.

If the dog is disapproved, he is returned, and the cheque is also returned.

The objections to this mode of procedure are several, and from both points of view. The buyer having returned the dog, may have some difficulty in regaining possession of his cheque if he is dealing with a dishonest person. On the other hand, the seller may be the victim, and may find that he has parted with his dog in exchange for a worthless piece of paper.

In the case, however, of a well-known man, the seller can with safety accept the cheque as security, but the sender must protect himself by writing the words "*Not Negotiable*" on the cheque ; otherwise the person in whose favour it is made out may pass it on to a third party, and if the drawer of the cheque should, scenting dishonesty afoot, stop payment of the cheque, the third party can proceed against him and recover the amount of the cheque, irrespective of the fact whether the dog sent was approved or not, while the man who sent the dog in the first place will probably have thought it wise to perform the vanishing act, or enquiries through one of the trade agencies may bring to light the fact that he is a man of straw, and not worth powder and shot. The words "*Not Negotiable*" stamped or written upon the cheque prevent a fraud of this kind, as the cheque not being negotiable security, only he in whose favour it has been made out can claim upon it, if the drawer thinks advisable to advise his bank to stop payment.

It is the height of folly to entrust one's money to perfect strangers residing at a considerable distance, on the assumption that one is dealing with a honest person. Nine times out of ten one may have no cause to regret it, but the tenth time may prove disastrous. It would also be the height of folly for a raw beginner to trust entirely to his own judgment, even though he may be theoretically perfect in his knowledge of a Bulldog, or may imagine himself to be. If he is fortunate enough to possess a friend in whose judgment he can rely, then he can easily obtain advice. Should he, however, not possess a friend with a knowledge of Bulldogs, his best plan would be to either make use of the services of one of the experts on the list of *The Bazaar, Exchange, and Mart*, which services are available to any one, and without charge ; or, should he be living in a district far removed from the residence of any one of these gentlemen, he would do well to write to the editor of one of the canine journals and ask from him the name and address of some reputable Bulldog owner and breeder residing in his district. He might then go to this gentleman and ask his advice, perhaps proffering a fee, which, however, would be refused in ninety-nine cases out of a hundred. In this way the beginner would secure himself against a very possible loss and great disappointment. It is practically certain he will meet with not a few disappointments in his subsequent career as a Bulldog owner, and if by some such simple method as those suggested here he can guard himself from being disappointed at the outset, he will be acting wisely.

"CORA."

Monarch.   Beauty.

Ch. Dimboola.   Liza 'Awkins.   Don Alexis.   Cameo.

Winner of Seven Firsts.

The property of

H. ST. JOHN COOPER.

CHAPTER II.

BULLDOG owners are well catered for in the matter of clubs, there being about a dozen clubs devoted to the interests of this breed in various parts of England, Scotland, and Ireland. First in age and foremost in importance is the Bulldog Club Incorporated, which has its headquarters in London, in which city it holds its annual exhibition of Bulldogs; but at almost any show of any magnitude that is held in the kingdom the Bulldog Club offers its valuable trophies and medals for competition among its own members. This club has a list of club judges, which are elected annually; and its special prizes are offered only at such shows where one or another of these club judges officiates.

The London Bulldog Society, originally known as the South London Bulldog Society, is another highly successful London organisation. Like the Bulldog Club Incorporated, it holds an annual show in London, and offers numerous special prizes for competition among its members at most of the more important shows where Bulldogs are catered for.

The third of the more important clubs is the British Bulldog Club, which was established twelve years ago. It practically has no headquarters, and its membership is drawn from all parts of the country. Its annual show is generally given in connection with some other dog society's exhibition, and is held in a different town every year. It offers special prizes to its members at most of the more important shows.

A prominent provincial club is the Birmingham and Midland Counties Bulldog Club, another the Manchester and District Bulldog Club.

The following is a list of the more important Bulldog Clubs

"KING PLUTO."

The property of
A. HURDLE, ESQ.,
16, SEATON AVENUE,
PLYMOUTH.

*Photo by Emeny and Sons,
Sudbury.*

of England, with the names and addresses of the Honorary Secretaries :—

The Bulldog Club Incorporated.   Mr. E. A. Vicary, 14, Park-holme Road, Dalston, London, N.

The London Bulldog Society.   Mr. W. J. Stubbs, Melbourne Cottage, Mitcham Road, Tooting, S.W.

The British Bulldog Club.   Mr. Cyril Jackson, Charterhouse, Teignmouth.

The Birmingham and Midland Counties Bulldog Club.   Mr. E. M. Brooke, Sutton Coldfield.

The Manchester and District Bulldog Club.   Mr. W. P. Kidd, Briar Cottage, Swinton, Manchester.

The Northumberland and Durham Bulldog Club.   Mr. L. Brown, 4, Lovaine Avenue, North Shields.

Besides these, there is a club in Scotland, and a club of the very first importance in New York.

The Standard of Points issued by the Bulldog Club, which exhaustively describes the formation of a perfect Bulldog, is deserving of the close study of the beginner.   It may be divided into five sections, namely, General Appearance, Head, Body, Weight, and Colour.

In General Appearance the Bulldog is a smooth-coated, thick-set dog, low in stature, particularly in front.   His chest is of great width, and he stands upon short but straight and very muscular forelegs.   In comparison, the hindquarters are higher and rather lightly made.   The head is exceedingly large and massive, the face very short, with broad muzzle inclining upwards, the body short and compact; and the impression that the dog should give is of great strength, massiveness, and withal activity.

The Skull must be very large in proportion to the size of the dog, the larger the better.   From the lower jaw to the apex of the skull it should be very high and also broad and square.   The forehead should be flat, the temples broad and prominent, causing a deep indention, called "the stop," between the eyes.

The Eyes should be situated low down in the skull, as far from the ears as possible; they should be far apart but yet situated quite in the front of the face; in shape they should be round, and very dark in colour, shewing no white when the dog is looking directly in front of him.

The Ears.—The correct form of ear is that known as "rose" ears, they should be set high on the head, and should be very small and thin; Bat, Tulip, and Button ears are all serious defects.

The Face should be as short as possible and closely wrinkled, the nose must be large and jet black, set well back almost between the eyes. The "chop" should be thick and pendulous, hanging well down over the underjaw on each side, but not in front. There should be an abundance of loose skin about the throat and neck.

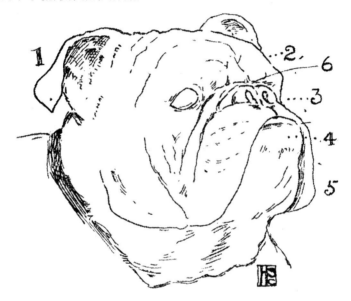

1 *Rose Ear.* 3 *Lay Back* . 5 *Flews*
2 *Temple.* 4 *Turn-up* . 6 *Stop* .

The Underjaw must be square and strong, and should project considerably beyond the upper jaw and turn upwards, with large and strong and even teeth.

The Chest must be very wide, round, prominent and deep, with slanting, deep, and very muscular shoulders.

The Body must be short and very strong, broad across the shoulders, but narrowing towards the loins; the back should have a distinct upward arch from behind the shoulders to the loins, which is very characteristic of the breed, and is called "Roach" back, or "Wheel" back.

The Tail must be set on low and carried straight down, never gaily; it should be rather short, thick at the root and tapering to a fine point. Screw tails are deformities, but are very common, and are not serious defects.

The Forelegs should be very stout, strong, and straight; they are short in proportion to the hindlegs and are set wide apart. The well-developed calves give the legs the appearance of being slightly bowed, but the bone should be perfectly straight; bandy or bent legs are defects.

The Colour.—There is a greater variety in the colouring of a Bulldog than in almost any other breed, viz., brindle, fawn or red, white, and the varieties or mixture of any two colours, such as brindle and white, fawn and white, etc.

The following colours are objectionable, though very rare:— black, slate, or blue, dark brown. The coat should be fine in texture, short and smooth.

The Feet should be very slightly turned out, the toes well split up and arched; splay or flat feet are serious objections.

The Weight.—The most desirable weight of a Bulldog is about forty-five pounds.

DEFECTS.

The Dudley Nose.—Prominent among objectionable points that are sometimes exhibited by specimens of the breed is what is termed the " Dudley " nose. There is no doubt but that at one time the Dudley or liver-coloured nose was a recognised Bulldog property, and was as common among the dogs as the black nose was rare. By careful breeding experiments, continued over a period of some thirty years, the Dudley nose has almost been bred out of existence, but not quite, however. It will often make its appearance when least expected, one puppy, for instance, being thus marked while all the others in the litter have noses of the correct colour. Dogs so mismarked are entirely valueless from a show point of view, though they are often used for breeding purposes : this is, however, not to be altogether recommended if the ultimate good of the breed is to be considered. As a matter of fact, however, Dudley bitches will oftentimes breed nothing but black-nosed stock ; and many a dog that has won honours on the show bench is the offspring of a Dudley dam. Still, if breeders have the good of the breed constantly in mind, they will not breed from Dudley-nosed dogs and bitches, and, in the course of time, it is possible that the objectionable colour may entirely disappear ; but possibly this is too much to expect from a man who possesses an otherwise good and useful bitch.

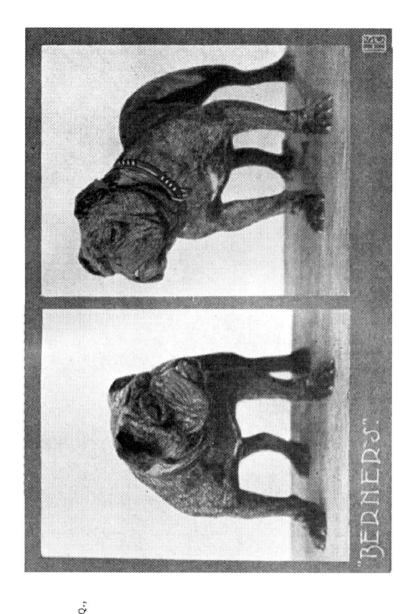

"BERNERS,"

The property of
G. W. RICHARDS, ESQ.,
GREENLANDS,
HEVER, KENT.

"BERNERS."

Photo by
H. St. John Cooper,
Brighton.

There is a popular belief that all Dudley dogs are particularly good in all other properties. The idea is, however, quite erroneous, the fact being that unless a Dudley dog is unusually good in other properties, his earthly career terminates at an early age ; he is, as a matter of fact, destroyed in his puppyhood unless he shows exceptional promise in other respects, and in that case is then often kept on for breeding purposes, or to sell to someone requiring a dog for a companion.

By a law made in 1884 by the Bulldog Club Incorporated, at a general meeting, and passed by ten votes for, to three against, Dudley-nosed dogs and bitches were excluded from competition at all shows. This resolution was confirmed later in the year at another general meeting, when the voting was twenty-eight for and eighteen against, though no record of this appears, as it should, in the Club's Standard. The Dudley Bulldog is thus entirely disqualified at shows, and it cannot be denied that, though this utter disqualification of a first-rate dog that is marred simply by the colour of his nose, is extremely severe, some such drastic method as this is necessary if the defect is ever to reach the vanishing point. It must not, however, be forgotten that it is breeding and not showing that is responsible for points good and bad ; and so long as Dudleys are bred from, so long will the colour crop up, to the disgust of the breeder.

Pinched Nostrils.—A serious defect in a Bulldog is a small nose and pinched nostril. It is a fault of the worst kind, for a dog with such a nose is unable to breathe properly, and would be quite incapable of performing the work that was once his reason for existence. Unfortunately there are far too many dogs with small, pinched noses and inadequate nostrils to be seen on the show benches ; and the beginner in Bulldogs will do well to carefully avoid the acquisition of a dog so malformed.

Ears.—Tulip ears are now very rarely met with in the Bulldog, though they are only too common among the toy variety of the breed. Buttoned ears, are, however, far more common, unfortunately, and, as a defect, are only less serious than a Dudley nose. A button ear is an ear that folds over and falls forward, so that when the dog is viewed from the front nothing of the inside of the ear is seen. Though the possession of button ears does not mean entire disqualification as in the case of the Dudley nose, dogs with this defect are severely handicapped, and rightly so. Heavy ears are a minor defect if the ears are carried properly. A Bulldog's ears should be fine, and thin, and small, and if large, thick, and coarse, are objectionable.

"INGOLDSBY LAWYER."

The property of
H. ST. JOHN COOPER, ESQ.,
OXBERRY, SURRENDEN ROAD,
BRIGHTON.

From the painting by Miss Monica Gray.

Jarrold & Sons, Ltd., Printers and Engravers, Norwich.

Eyes.—If a Bulldog shows the whites of his eyes when he is viewed from the front, he is sometimes called terrier-eyed. It detracts much from the dog's appearance, and is another minor defect.

Skull.—The skull of the Bulldog should be flat and the temples broad and prominent. A round skull is defective.

Face.—Sometimes a Bulldog is called "Down-faced;" this means that the nose is not sufficiently set back, and there is too great a length from its tip to a line drawn from eye to eye. An up-faced dog is a dog which has its nose set well back, and has a strong, upward sweep of underjaw.

MR. H. ST. JOHN COOPER'S LATE

"INGOLDSBY LAWYER."

Underjaw.—"Frog-face" is an expression often used to denote a want of underjaw. This is, however, not quite correct. A frog-faced Bulldog, properly, is a dog that is somewhat deficient in underjaw, and who also possesses a pair of goggling

CHAMPION "PRINCE ALBERT."

The property of
    LUKE CRABTREE, ESQ.,
    LEA GRANGE, BLACKLEY,
    MANCHESTER.

eyes, which gives him a peculiarly frog-like appearance ; need-less to say this is a defect of the worst kind. A straight under-jaw, though it may protrude considerably beyond the upper jaw, is a defect, but far worse is an underjaw that is overshot by the upper jaw.

Lack of wrinkle is termed " Tight-skin ; " this and the lack of size in the skull are defects. The average size of a Bulldog's skull should be, taking the dog's weight into consideration, from seventeen inches to twenty inches, measuring above the temples and drawing the measure tight. Very few dogs indeed go more than twenty inches round the skull, though very often dogs may appear to possess a much larger skull than they really have. Champion Boomerang, probably the best dog of modern times, had, apparently, an enormous skull, but its strict measurement was nineteen inches.

Other defects to be looked for and guarded against are want of bone, too great a height on the forelegs, bowed or bandy forelegs, insufficient depth of brisket, wrong formation of shoulder and of elbow, flat sides and want of roundness of rib, a long and gaily carried tail, a thick coarse tail with long hair, a dipped back, and splay feet.

Tails.—There is a wide diversity of opinion on the subject of tails. Some, especially American fanciers, pin their faith to a screwed tail, whilst many of the older fanciers in this country strongly object to this un-Bulldog-like appendage. Undoubtedly the screw tail is due to a Pug cross, and for this reason it is not approved of by serious Bulldog men. The crank tail is a tail otherwise straight, but ornamented by a kink, or possibly two ; this is also considered desirable by very many. The pump-handle tail needs no description, and is the tail that is usually to be seen in prints of the old-fashioned fighting Bulldog. The ideal tail, however, is that which is described by the Standard of the Bulldog Club. It is set on low and carried straight downwards. It is perfectly straight, thick at the root and tapering to a fine point. Its length should be about six inches, a little more or a little less. It should be entirely free of thick and coarse hair. It should not be as thick at the tip as it is at the root, nor should it be possible for the dog to " get it up ; " such is the tail that all breeders might strive to secure.

Feet.—Splay feet and "down on the pasterns" is often, if not always due to want of proper exercise during puppyhood. Weakness of bone and rickety limbs are often due to the same reason, and also to improper feeding and bad housing.

A rough, staring coat is most frequently due to the presence

of worms in the intestines, which are often responsible also for
fœtid breath and irritation of the skin.

Expression.—A defect of very considerable magnitude, is
the want of a proper Bulldog expression, as has before been
pointed out.   A dog may possess a great number of the
necessary points, yet lacking a true Bulldog expression, he fails
to be a good dog.   The true Bulldog expression is almost in-
describable, and no dog of modern times possessed it in such a
marked degree as did Champion Boomerang, who was bred by
Mr. Williams, and owned until his death by Mr. Luke Crabtree,
of Blackley, Manchester, by whose courtesy the portrait of this
famous dog appears in these pages.

A Study in Bulldog expression.

MR. LUKE CRABTREE'S LATE

CHAMPION "BOOMERANG."

Courage, even ferocity, combined with intelligence and honesty
—sourness is perhaps the word that best describes the expression,
yet it is the sourness of aloofness rather than the sourness of
ill-temper, a sourness that in a human being would probably
be described as haughtiness.

CHAPTER III.

THE BROOD BITCH—SHOW BITCHES AND BROOD BITCHES—SUIT-
ABLE MATING—THE AGE AT WHICH TO BREED—PEDIGREE—
THE STUD DOG.

It is safe to assume that in nine cases out of ten the initial
purchase will be that of a brood bitch, and the intending breeder
will do well to give the most careful thought and consideration
to the selection of a suitable animal. If he is favoured by
fortune, the bitch will in due course have puppies, and these
puppies, which will be bred from in their turn, will form the
nucleus of a kennel that may in time become famous. The first
brood bitch that the beginner purchases may therefore be
regarded in the light of the foundation-stone of the kennel, and
on her very much will depend. If she is a bitch of bad type,
lacking Bulldog character, wanting in bone, stamina, and many
of the necessary points, the beginning will prove a very bad one,
and a few extra pounds spent at the outset in the acquisition of
a better stamp of bitch will be money well laid out.

It is not, however, always a question of money. Sometimes a
really good brood bitch may be bought for a very inconsiderable
amount, or possibly she may be purchased in her puppyhood
with the idea of breeding from her when she matures. This
course, however, is not one altogether to be recommended to the
tyro, and for the following reason. It is better that he should
commence operations in the possession of a bitch that has
proved herself to be a breeder and a good mother. More trouble
and danger is usually experienced at the breeding of a first litter
than at subsequent litters, and it would be well, therefore, for the
breeder who lacks experience not to set himself too difficult a
task at the outset. If the bitch herself possesses the experience
that her owner lacks, the way will be smoothed to a certain
extent. The instinct of animals is always wonderful, and never
more so than in the case of a young animal that is for the first

time bringing her young into the world. Nature prompts her to perform the various necessary duties in a manner which to the more helpless human being is nothing short of miraculous. But there are exceptions, and unfortunately young Bull-bitches in some instances do not seem to be endowed with the sense and instinct that is common enough with less carefully bred dogs. And sometimes even when instinct prompts certain acts, the bitch is physically unable to perform them. This is particularly the case with a Bull-bitch, who, owing to the formation of her underjaw, is often unable to bite through the umbilical cord, an operation that an even-jawed terrier can perform with ease.

The advice on this subject given by "Great Dane" (Mr. R. E. Nicholas) in his admirable work, "The Principles of Dog Breeding,"* is of such value to the beginner that it is reproduced here in full :—

"At the very outset of his career as a breeder the novice is confronted with the problem of how best to make a beginning —whether to start with puppies or matured dogs. On the one hand he finds that well-bred puppies cost less than equally well-bred bitches, and he also anticipates the natural delight in shaping their dispositions, and in so building up their bodies and constitutions by judicious feeding and care as to ensure their begetting the healthiest possible progeny in due time. On the other hand, matured brood bitches would evidently yield quicker results, but he feels that they could never be quite as much to him as if they had grown up, and grown good, under his own hand, so to speak. Reasoning thus, and tacitly assuming that well-bred and well-nourished puppies necessarily develop into desirable dogs, the beginner who is not unduly covetous of rapid monetary returns, generally decides in favour of the puppies, and so decides wrongly, for the chief of the premises on which his decision is based is altogether wrong and misleading. The man of experience—the practical breeder who has himself suffered from the same mistake, or has seen it made by others—would have told him that puppies are a veritable lottery, with many chances but few prizes ; that probably not one in a thousand of the best-bred fulfils its owner's hopes ; that their ultimate value as breeding stock cannot be estimated by the most expert judges, while one may, at any rate, approximately, gauge the worth of a matured animal ; and that though the

* "The Principles of Dog Breeding," by "Great Dane." 1s. Toogood & Sons, Southampton.

"MOSTON MAJOR."

The property of
LUKE CRABTREE, ESQ.,
LEA GRANGE, BLACKLEY,
MANCHESTER.

immediate outlay may be greater, it is both safer and more satis·
factory to choose adult bitches which have bred once or twice,
and are yet young enough to bear profitably for some years."

It is better, therefore, that the beginner should start with a
bitch that has bred at least one litter, and as he gains in
experience so can he afford in time to brave the dangers of
breeding from younger and less-seasoned stock.

Brood Bitches and Show Bitches.—With many breeds
there is no marked difference between bitches that are exhibited
and those that are kept for breeding purposes. The show terrier-
bitch can be bred from with as little risk as can a bitch that is
not fit for show, but in the case of Bulldogs it is different.

The very points that would qualify a Bull-bitch for high
honours on the show bench, render her quite unfit to become
a mother. A show bitch should be short in the back, and
compact; indeed, the shorter she is in back the better, but if an
attempt is made to breed from her the result would usually
prove disastrous. As the show bitch is short and compact, so
is the brood bitch large-framed and roomy. She must have
room to carry her puppies naturally, and give birth to them
without endangering her own life.

Points.—But, at the same time, though the breeder may have
no intention of exhibiting the bitch, he must yet look to find
in her most of those points that he hopes to see reproduced
in the puppies, and, more important still, he must satisfy himself
that she comes of a strain, or family, which has been responsible
for the production of excellent dogs of good type. Though
possibly the brood bitch may herself be inclined to plainness,
yet, if she comes of good typical and healthy stock, she will, if
suitably mated, throw, in all probability, excellent and desirable
puppies.

No glaring fault, however, should be permitted in the brood
bitch, for no matter how excellent her pedigree may be, there
is a grave possibility of her passing on the objectionable feature
to her progeny. First and foremost she must be healthy, healthy
both in body and in mind. She must be free of all internal
growths, diseased organs, and skin diseases; moreover, she
should be good-tempered and tractable, a bitch that is easy to
handle, for an ill-tempered bitch generally becomes absolutely
savage when she has young with her, and the novice's difficulties
are thereby increased a hundredfold.

Her bone must be massive and strong, without the slightest
inclination to rickets; in short, on no account must she be a

"MOSTON MICHAEL."

The property of
    LUKE CRABTREE, ESQ.,
    LEA GRANGE, BLACKLEY,
    MANCHESTER.

cripple, but must be thoroughly sound in both limb and wind. The smaller and finer her ears, and the broader and more upturned her underjaw, the better. She should have a big, black nose, and as many of the points laid down by the Standard as it is possible to get.

From this the beginner will perhaps imagine that a brood bitch should be practically a show bitch in all things save in the extra length of back and roominess, and, to a certain extent, he will be right, for the better the individual bitch is, the better the chance of obtaining good puppies.

Too much should not be looked for from the dog. Many breeders are under the impression that so long as the sire is desirable in every way, the quality of the bitch herself matters little. This is, however, an entirely erroneous belief, and it is certain that the mating together of a first-class dog and bitch of first-class family tradition should assuredly result in the production of first-class puppies; while if only one parent is good and the other of indifferent quality, the puppies will probably be a mixed lot of uncertain type, and, consequently, when they arrive at maturity they will have no particular type to impress upon their own offspring. Therefore, when the question of expense is one that must be studied carefully, the beginner will be doing well if he decides on the purchase of one really first-rate bitch, in preference to two or more of less quality.

Certain minor defects may, however, be forgiven the brood bitch, always provided these defects are not inherited by her. The operations of the conscientious breeder must be entirely based upon a close study of the laws of inheritance.

Pedigree.—The study of pedigree is essential to consistent successful breeding, but it is not sufficient by any means that the breeder has at the tip of his tongue the names of parents, grandparents, great-grandparents, and so on for generations. He must know a great deal more than this. He must know the family traditions—that is, the general attributes of the animals from whom his bitch is descended. He must discover in what points those animals usually excelled, and in which points they were as a rule deficient; and, always bearing this in mind, he should search for a suitable mate for his bitch, and endeavour to build up a strain in which the defective points are rarely, if ever, seen.

Suitable Mating.—The expression suitable mating has been used more than once, and it is now well to describe what suitable mating really is. In breeding, the laws of inheritance must always be taken into account. It is by no means sufficient that a dog possesses certain good points which the breeder is desirous of securing for his puppies, it is necessary for him to inquire into the dog's ancestry and learn if the good points are hereditary ones or merely the result of a freak of nature, which has produced a good dog, as she sometimes does, from bad or indifferent stock. Those points that the bitch is herself deficient in, the breeder must look for in the dog that he proposes to mate with her, but he must assure himself that these qualities are the dog's by inheritance.

The best plan the novice can pursue is to first decide what strain or family it is better to mate his bitch with. Let him choose the family first and the individual dog afterwards, and let him look for the main characteristics of that family in the dog himself.

As an illustration, we will suppose that a bitch otherwise of good quality has a pair of heavy, badly carried ears, and that heavy and badly carried ears is a trait in the strain from which she is bred. His first thought must be to ascertain what particular strain of Bulldog has had consistently good ears ; in short, in what particular strain good ears are the rule and poor ones the exception. Having discovered this, he will then set about finding a dog bred from this strain who is himself a good-eared animal. He will then know that by mating his bitch with this dog he is doing all that is possible to eradicate the undesirable point.

With ears, so with other points, and while individual excellence should always be looked for, the cause of that excellence should not be forgotten.

It must also be remembered that bad points are as faithfully reproduced as good ones, and if the dog has not only the good points that are necessary to counteract the bad ones possessed by the bitch, but bad ones of his own as well, and bad ones that have been inherited by him, then he should be discarded in favour of the dog whose good points may possibly not be quite so prominent, but who, at any rate, has no glaring faults that may be reproduced in the puppies.

Age at which to Breed.—Much has been said and written on the subject of breeding from immature bitches, and it is certain that those who are opposed to breeding from a bitch at her first heat have a strong argument in favour of their opinion. A bitch usually comes into use at the age of from nine months to eleven months, generally speaking during the tenth month, and at this age she is of course in an undeveloped state ; she is still in her puppyhood, and all the vitality she possesses, and the nourishment she can assimilate, is required to build up her own

CHAMPION "BROADLEA SQUIRE."

The property of
    J. W. PROCTER, ESQ.,
    WARFORD HOUSE,
    MOBBERLEY.

frame, and if she is called upon to undertake the duties of maternity while she is herself still in an immature state, the effects must be disastrous to her own future development and constitution ! This undoubtedly holds good in the case of the larger breeds of dogs, such as the St. Bernard, the Great Dane, and the Mastiff. But in the opinion of the writer, an opinion that he knows is shared by the majority of Bulldog breeders, not only is it advisable, but it is of very great advantage to breed from a Bull bitch at her first heat.

A bitch that is bred from while she herself is still in her puppy-hood, gives birth to her puppies with greater ease by reason of the greater elasticity of her bones, which have not yet firmly set, and the birth of this first litter makes the way clear to a certain extent to future litters. It will generally, in fact it may be said it will always, be found that the bitch who suffers the least at the time of whelping and requires the least assistance, is she who has been bred from at her first heat.

Moreover, in the case of Bull-bitches—and the reader must remember that the writer is referring to no other breed of dog—young bitches as a rule very greatly improve after the birth of their first litter. The quite understandable and reasonable argument of those who are opposed to early breeding does not apparently hold good in the case of Bull-bitches, though undoubtedly it does in the case of animals that are required to attain great size, such as bitches of the breeds before mentioned. If a bitch is fit to breed from at all, let her be bred from at her first heat.

So far we have in this matter only concerned ourselves with the bitch herself, but what of the puppies that have been bred from immature bitches?

There is a well-known rule in poultry breeding, and that is that first-year pullets must be mated with cocks in the second or third year, for the mating together of pullets and cockerels will result in the production of unfertile eggs, or of small and weedy chickens.

The same rule holds good with dog breeding. If the bitch is young and immature, the dog must be thoroughly matured and of good age ; while on the contrary, if an old bitch is to be bred from, the younger the dog the better. Age should be on one side.

A recent breeding experience of the writer's may not be out of place here. He mated two young bitches—litter sisters at the age of ten months (their first heat)—with a dog of six years of age. One bitch gave birth to ten puppies, the other to nine. In neither case did the bitch experience the least trouble in bringing the puppies into the world. The puppies were all born alive, and flourished exceedingly, while the bitches both had a plentiful supply of milk, and proved the best of mothers. One bitch unfortunately contracted distemper soon after the birth of her puppies, and succumbed, but the other has progressed more rapidly during the few months that have elapsed since she gave birth to her puppies than might have been expected, judging by her previous progress, and has improved almost out of recognition. Such is the writer's experience of breeding from immature stock.

Œstrum.—The actual time for mating a bitch with a dog is during the period of œstrum or heat, which usually occurs at intervals of six months.

The first appearance of this period is generally noticeable by an enlarging and swelling of the sexual organ. After a lapse of a day or two a thin blood-coloured discharge from the vagina is to be seen. This discharge generally lasts for from nine to ten days. When the discharge ceases the time has come to mate the bitch.

The entire period of œstrum usually lasts over three weeks, and as a rule it is admitted that the nearer the end of the period the bitch is mated the better for her chance of proving in whelp. But at the same time the period should not be allowed to advance too far. Two services should usually be allowed, the first two days after the cessation of the discharge, and the second three or four days later. If a third at a still later period can be arranged for, so much the better.

At this time the bitch should be kept quiet, her diet should be light and somewhat varied, excess of heating, starchy, and fat food should not be allowed. She should at all times, except immediately after service, have plenty of fresh water within her reach, though she must never be allowed to enter water at such a time, and she should receive a little gentle exercise every day.

Railway Journeys.—The practice of sending a bitch on a long railway journey for the purpose of being mated, is one to be avoided when possible. During the period of œstrum, the nature of many bitches undergoes a complete temporary change. An animal usually quiet often becomes excitable and sometimes the most docile and even-tempered becomes snappish and quarrelsome. If a bitch is sent a railway journey at this time, the unusual noise and bustle upsets her, and by the time she arrives at her journey's end she is not in a satisfactory condition to be mated. In cases

"WILSID."

The property of
    W. P. KIDD, ESQ.,
    BRIAR COTTAGE,
    SWINTON,
    MANCHESTER.

when a railway journey is imperative, such as when a bitch is being sent to visit a certain dog that is particularly desirable as a sire, she should, if possible, be accompanied by an attendant, or by her master ; at any rate by someone with whose face and voice she is familiar. If this is a course that cannot be pursued, then arrangements should be made with the owner of the stud dog, by which the bitch is sent at least some three or four days before the time for service. She will thus be able to get over the excitement of the journey and settle down quietly before she is visited by the dog, and after the services have taken place she should be allowed to remain another day or two in her temporary home. If more care was taken in this direction, these visits would usually prove more fertile and less disappointing to the owner, who has not only wasted the amount of the stud fee and railway expenses, but has also to wait another six months before his bitch is in season again.

When a thoroughly suitable mate can be found in the immediate neighbourhood, so much the better, but the owner of a bitch should not be content to mate her with a dog solely because the latter lives in the same street. It is better indeed to risk the possible disappointment of sending the bitch by train, to visit the suitable dog, knowing that if she does prove in whelp there is every reason to expect that her puppies will be good ones.

Stud Dog.—When a man is able to keep more than some two or three dogs, he will do wisely if he invests in a really high-class stud dog, but in such a case the order of things must be reversed, and, possessing the dog, he must select his bitches with a view to their fitness to be mated with the dog.

A successful stud dog need not of necessity be a successful show dog, indeed some of the most successful sires have had little or no claim to be considered first-rate specimens of their breed. If the family history of these dogs, however, is inquired into, it will generally—invariably—be found that they are descended from carefully bred stock of general excellence. In all probability the names of some noted winners will appear in the pedigree, and though the dog himself seems to have inherited but few of the good points that made his forefathers famous, yet he is capable of impressing these same good points on his own offspring. On the other hand there are many exceptionally good dogs, dogs that have won under the most critical judges in the biggest and best shows, who at stud have proved to be utter failures. What is the reason? It is simply this. Such dogs are mere freaks, they are the lucky flukes that have made their appearance in the world without any particular reason. They are not the result of careful and systematic breeding; no honour and glory is due to their breeders, who have produced them simply by sheer luck, and as these dogs have not been carefully, systematically, and scientifically bred for, they are more often than not quite incapable of passing on their good points to their immediate offspring.

Thus while a good stud dog need not always be a good show dog, the reverse also holds good, and a good show dog does not always prove himself a good stud dog. But the novice must not at once jump to the conclusion that no show dog can make a good sire. The reverse of this has been and is being constantly proved. There are many good dogs who owe their good quality to a systematic breeding for good points, persisted in by breeders for generation after generation. These good dogs are the results which have crowned their efforts ; and such animals as these are invaluable to the breed which they ornament. For the purposes of the breeder, however, it may be taken that the value of a stud dog, like that of a brood bitch, lies not in his own quality, but in the quality of the puppies he begets. Hence it will be seen that the successful stud dog must be well-bred, and by " well-bred " is understood that he is the outcome of systematic and scientific breeding operations. He must be healthy, and he must be absolutely sound in wind and limb. Too many crippled dogs are bred from, and too many weedy, crippled, and undesirable puppies are the result. A sound dog is as essential as a sound bitch, and if stock is not sound it is not worth the keeping.

CHAPTER IV.

WHELPING—PERSONAL ATTENDANCE—THE NEED FOR A FOSTER-MOTHER—EXCHANGING PUPPIES—FOOD AND EXERCISE FOR THE SUCKLING BITCH.

THE period of gestation in the bitch is sixty-three days, and at the time she receives her first service from the dog, a count should be made so that the breeder will know when to expect her to whelp, should she prove. Thus if a bitch is served for the first time on a Monday, the breeder will anticipate her whelping on the sixty-third day—*i.e.* the Monday of the ninth week from the time of her service. It is possible however that a bitch may not prove to the first service, but to the second which has taken place some days later, or even to the third later still ; yet the breeder will know that she will have her puppies about the time he anticipates, and will make his preparations accordingly.

Gestation.—During the early days of gestation there will be little or no apparent change in the bitch ; she may with safety be allowed to live her usual life, and may take her exercise with the other dogs, if there be any. As the time goes on, and she begin to show signs of pregnancy, which signs are usually visible at about the fifth or sixth week, and in some cases long before this, as early even as the third week, she must receive a little extra care and attention. In the first place she must be separated from the other dogs and allowed a kennel to herself ; her exercise should be curtailed but not stopped, for a little gentle exercise every day is highly beneficial, indeed necessary to her. Her food must be light and nourishing, the usual quantity may be slightly increased, and the quality improved, for it must be remembered that she has not only herself to nourish but the puppies which she is bearing as well.

As the time progresses towards the eighth week, she should be kept much to herself, away from other dogs, and if she is heavy

"ST. AMANT."

The property of
    DR. GROSART WELLS
    ST. ALBANS.

Photo by F. Usher, Esq., St. Albans.

in whelp, care must be taken to prevent her from springing up to, or jumping down from, high places.

Her sleeping bed should be in the form of a large and shallow tray or box, into which she can step without any exertion. Exercising should continue throughout the whole of the period, but towards the end should be of a gentle nature, and it is usually safer to take the bitch out by herself on the lead to guard against any sudden and violent activity on her part.

So long as the bitch is willing and anxious for exercise she should be indulged, but at the first sign of unwillingness to leave her kennel, no force or more gentle persuasion should be used to combat her desire for rest.

This desire is usually the first sign of approaching puppy-birth.

Quietude is now essential, and the bitch must be left to herself and fed and watched by her usual attendant.

One of the surest signs of the immediate approach of labour, is the growing uneasiness of the bitch. She will commence by scratching away the straw, so as to leave a nest with the boards of the box laid bare.

After this manifestation, whelping may be looked for immediately, certainly within the hour, and the owner or keeper will do well now to keep the bitch under constant observation ; yet, at the same time he should not worry her with officious and unnecessary attention.

When the bitch has scratched the straw away, it is usually well to remove it entirely, leaving her in the empty box. Some breeders are in the habit of putting a strip of old carpet or a sack in the bottom of the box, but unless this is tacked down the bitch will scratch this to one side also. The better plan is to leave her in the empty box.

The attendant will now provide himself with a soft towel, a large rough cloth, and a pair of sharp scissors for which he may, or may not, have any use.

Whelping.—If the bitch gives birth to the puppies without trouble it will be found, as the puppies come away, that they are enveloped in a thin elastic membrane, which the bitch will proceed to rip open with her teeth ; but should she fail in this duty, the attendant must at once make an opening to allow the ingress of air to the newly born puppy, which is attached to the placenta or afterbirth by means of the umbilical cord. The usual practice of all healthy bitches is to devour the afterbirth and bite off the cord, so freeing the puppy, but sometimes, and more especially in the case of a young bitch breeding for the first time, she does not always perform this duty, when it will be necessary for the attendant to cut the cord through with the scissors and remove the afterbirth from the box.

The cord should be severed about six inches away from the puppy, and the piece that is left attached to the puppy will in the course of twenty-four hours or so dry up and fall off. Never on any account must the cord be cut close to the puppy, or severe bleeding and probably death will be the result.

Some breeders make a practice of tying the cord before cutting it as a preventative to bleeding, but if ample length of cord is left to the puppy this tying is not necessary.

The box should now be roughly dried with the cloth, and the puppy, which must be very gently handled, should be rapidly dried with the soft towel and returned to the bitch if she shows the slightest anxiety for its company, as in ninety-nine cases out of a hundred she will.

Should, however, labour be difficult and prolonged, and the bitch in great pain, the puppies as they are born may be placed in a basket containing flannel and stood near a fire or stove, if the weather should happen to be cold. Except in such difficult cases, however, it is always better to allow the puppies to stay with the dam.

As the puppies are born, the box should be roughly cleaned and dried with the rough cloth, until the entire litter has been delivered.

A second box, which has been previously prepared by tacking a piece of sacking or old carpet to the bottom, is now brought to the kennel, and the mother and puppies transferred to it, when they may be left to settle down.

When a bitch is difficult to handle, however, she may be left with the puppies in the first box, which the attendant will dry as much as possible, but it is better when possible to make the exchange and remove the box in which the whelping has taken place entirely.

If the whelping is very prolonged—and more often than not it may occupy anything from three to twelve hours, the bitch should be given a little thin oatmeal gruel, or Mellin's food, to sustain her, and if she is evidently suffering much pain a few drops of brandy or gin may be added to the gruel or administered in a little water. In the absence of any severe pains no spirit should be given.

For the first twenty-four hours after whelping the bitch should be fed entirely on light and sloppy and easily digested food, and there is nothing better for the purpose than Mellin's food, which should be prepared as the manufacturers direct.

"KILBURN PRESIDENT."

The property of
H. SCHALFERMAN, ESQ.,
112, GOLDHAWK ROAD,
LONDON.

She may also partake of a little beef tea. That manufactured by the Plasmon Company is particularly valuable for this purpose, while a little of the Plasmon powder, or jelly made from the Plasmon powder, may with advantage be added to the Mellin's food, or the gruel, for although the stomach must not be given too much work to do, the strength of the animal must be maintained, and easily digested and strength-giving foods are particularly valuable at this time. In all probability, it will be found that the bitch has given birth to more puppies than she can with comfort bring up; a Bull-bitch may have anything from one to ten or even twelve puppies at one litter, the average number being seven or eight.

The Foster-Mother.—Four puppies are as many as a bitch may be entrusted with in safety, for though she may have sufficient milk for more, there is during the earlier days great danger to be anticipated from her laying on the little ones and crushing them to death.

The lighter and more agile fox terrier is by no means so great an offender in this respect as is the Bull-bitch, for the Bulldog is comparatively a clumsy breed, and at no time is the clumsiness more apparent than at this.

Hence it will be seen that the services of a foster-mother are not only desirable but absolutely necessary in the case of a Bull-bitch who is apparently about to have a large litter. Foster-mothers, which are usually bitches of mongrel parentage, can be obtained from either private persons who advertise in the canine journals, or from one or other of the several firms who make the supply of foster-mothers their business. Messrs. Marsh, of Wellingborough, state that they are prepared to supply foster-mothers for anything from toy puppies to lion cubs at a moment's notice, and a wire to this firm will generally result in the arrival of a foster-mother as fast as steam can bring her.

But it is better for the breeder not to put off this very necessary operation until the eleventh hour. He should arrange for the foster-mother at least a week before she is required, and will stipulate that she is due to whelp either at the same time as the Bull-bitch, or for preference a day or two days before. The foster-mother with her newly born puppies should therefore be already in the immediate neighbourhood.

Changing Puppies.—About four of her own puppies should be left with the foster-mother, and when the time comes to put the Bull-puppies on her the operation may be performed in the following manner: The Bull-puppies should be filched away one at a time from their mother, her attention being attracted in a contrary direction, so that she is not aware of what is taking place. The puppy is then carried to the foster-mother, whose attention is also distracted, a rapid exchange is then made, the Bull-puppy taking the place of a mongrel puppy, which is at once handed over to the executioner.

The attendant will stay with the foster-mother until he assures himself that she has taken to the stranger. When a bitch is procured that has fostered before, very little trouble is experienced, as a rule, in making this exchange, but sometimes a bitch may show a strong objection to the new-comer.

It is then merely a question of patience. A little milk from her teats should be smeared over the Bull-puppy, and it should be put to her again. If she even then objects to its presence, her own and the Bull-puppy should be taken from her entirely, and she should be kept alone until the incoming milk makes her uneasy ; she will then be allowed to return to the puppies, when she will usually take to her own and the stranger alike.

There is a more brutal and therefore more objectionable method of attaining the same end, which very few will care to indulge in.

The foster-puppy instead of being drowned is killed and cut open, and the Bull-puppy smeared with the blood; it is then placed with the mother, who, recognising the scent of her own offspring, allows the presence of the stranger. Very little can, however, be said in favour of this proceeding, as the same end can be attained by allowing the puppies to lie together, or by smearing the new-comer with the foster-mother's milk.

When it is seen that the foster-mother is licking the new arrival, it may be taken as a sign that all is well. So one by one the exchange is made, until at last all the foster's own puppies have been removed and she is sharing with the Bull-bitch the latter's litter.

Haste in making the exchange should be avoided unless the foster-mother is of a peculiarly amiable disposition. And henceforth the treatment of the foster-mother will be identical with the treatment of the Bull-bitch.

An erroneous idea is prevalent among certain people that the milk of a mongrel foster-mother is likely to impair the quality of the pure-bred puppies that she suckles. There is as much sense in this as there is in the supposition that to give young puppies newly laid eggs will cause them to grow up resembling hens.

Bedding.—Straw, the usual bedding for dogs, is not suitable as a bedding for newly-born puppies. Straw is far too hard and irritating, and for the first four or five days of their existence

"KILBURN KING."

The property of
H. SCHLAFERMAN, ESQ.,
112, GOLDHAWK ROAD,
SHEPHERD'S BUSH,
LONDON.

there is nothing better than a good dry sack or piece ot old carpet, which has been tightly tacked down to the bottom of the box. If the sack or carpet is not tacked, the bitch will most probably scratch it up, and one or other of the puppies getting under the folds may be crushed to death by the dam laying on it. After the fourth or fifth day, a little dry hay that has been carefully picked over forms a good bed ; but it will usually be found that the bitch much prefers the bare boards, and will scratch the hay away around the sides of the box. The box itself in which the bitch whelps, and in which she is to bring up her puppies, must be roomy, and should be square rather than oblong in shape, so that no matter which way the bitch lays the puppies can get to her easily. A good size for a Bull-bitch is from two feet six square to three feet square, the sides being about seven inches high.

Food.—The food of the bitch while she is suckling her young should be as nourishing as possible. In the ordinary course an adult dog is fed once or perhaps twice a day ; but the nursing bitch will require more generous treatment. Four meals a day will not be too many for her, and the quality of the food given should be of the highest standard.

The first meal of the day, which should be given as early as possible, should consist of porridge made with Quaker Oats (which require less boiling than the ordinary meal), or of Mellin's food with milk.

At mid-day a meal of raw lean meat is the best possible thing, and this may be followed by more of the milk food. After the first week or ten days her evening meal may be much the same as at ordinary times. Cleaned and well-boiled paunch, cut up and given with a little soaked hound meal or Melox is excellent, so, too, is fish (care being taken that there are no dangerous bones). Sheep's head with Melox or Rodnim soaked in the broth forms another dish that the bitch will take with avidity. But it must always be remembered, now and at all other times, that no small and dangerous bones, such as those found in the sheep's head, rabbits, poultry, fish, or game, are allowed to find their way into the dog's platter.

The last meal at night may be the same as the first given in the morning ; and this diet may be continued with changes until the time has come to wean the puppies, which is usually when they have arrived at the age of six weeks.

From the tenth to the fourteenth day the puppies will open their eyes ; at about the end of the fourth week they will show a desire to share their mother's food with her. Some bitches show a strong objection to hospitality of this kind, and will often snap at the puppies when they crowd into her dish. It is well, therefore, to feed the bitch outside the kennel from about the fourth week onward, though some are so gentle that they may be left with the puppies without fear. When the puppies show an inclination to lap, they may be given a little milk (undiluted), to which a little Plasmon has been added to bring it up to the strength of the bitch's milk, which is far stronger and more nourishing than cow's milk. At the fifth week, Mellin's food will be found most useful, as it will when the puppies are entirely weaned from their dam.

Exercise for the Suckling Bitch.—During the first few days after whelping, the bitch will show no inclination to leave her puppies as a rule; and if she does, the inclination should not be fostered. After about the third day she should be allowed to have a run in the yard for ten minutes or so at a time; and as the time goes on, the periods of her absence from her puppies may be slightly increased, until the fourth week, when she may be taken out for a little exercise. During the fifth week, she may be kept away from her puppies for an hour or so at a time—in fact, during the greater part of the day, allowing her to return to them at intervals, in order that she may suckle them. At the expiration of the sixth week, they may be entirely weaned from her, but if the weather is very cold or inclement, it is usually, well to allow her to sleep with them at night, unless she shows a strong disinclination for their society. If she does, she can hardly be blamed, for the teeth of puppies of six weeks old are like needle points, and her objection can easily be understood.

CHAPTER V.

THE breeder who aspires to produce sound and healthy stock must bear in mind the fact that rational feeding is not even second to rational mating. It is now a generally understood and accepted fact that the better bred a dog is the better food it requires, and while the cur can live and thrive on the hardest of fare, and even garbage that it picks up in the gutter, the dog of breeding would find it quite beyond its powers to sustain life on such a diet, but would in all probability succumb to an attack of gastritis, due to eating the filth on which a cur dog can maintain life.

With the canine race, so with the human. In the late South African war many of our soldiers succumbed to enteric fever, brought on in most cases through drinking impure water. Now these men, under their normal home conditions, were used to the comparatively pure water supplied by the water companies, and were thus unable to drink the foul water with impunity. Residents in the country can, however, vouch for the truth of the statement that gipsies are in the habit of drinking water from the foulest stagnant ponds, water which to other people would probably mean death, but which is harmless to them owing to the fact that for generations their constitutions have been accustomed to the hardest and roughest fare, impure water, and insanitary conditions of life generally. In the earlier days in England, before the advent of Water Companies and Sanitary Inspectors, there is no doubt that disease was less rife than it is at the present, and this is due to the fact that for generations the constitutions of the people had been hardened by a mode of living which to the present century man of normal civilised habits would be impossible. Therefore, while the mongrel dog may eat the filth and garbage of the gutter, and lap up foul water with impunity, the dog descended from a line of well-bred and

"UXBRIDGE MORGAN."

"MISS AUBREY."

The property of

W. R. GOODWIN, ESQ.,

SPRING COTTAGE, OXTED, SURREY,

AND KEARNEY, P.O., ONTARIO, CANADA.

well-nourished animals would be utterly unable to support life under such circumstances.

Good food is essential to good results in breeding, practically as essential as good blood, and the dog owner cannot give this part of his duties too much attention, nor study it too closely.

Meat is essential to the well-being of a dog. Naturally a carnivorous animal, his instinct is to eat meat, and it is generally safe to follow natural instincts.

Many writers, and among them men of undoubted ability and experience, advocate either a diet in which meat takes no part at all, or in some cases the withholding of meat from young stock until it arrives at the age of six or eight months.

In the opinion of the writer, an opinion shared by many experienced fanciers and dog owners, the withholding of meat from young stock is the greatest possible mistake. If at any time in its life a dog requires nourishing, it is at that period when it is building up its frame.

Meat in moderation may be given with advantage to young puppies that have just left their dams ; sparingly and judiciously at first. At six weeks the puppy may have a little raw lean beef, finely scraped or passed through a mincing machine ; about half an ounce or a little more per diem, increasing the quantity gradually. At three months it can have from four to six ounces, and puppies so reared will be found to be hardier, better nourished, and less prone to disease than those that are kept entirely on a starchy diet, which neither during puppyhood nor at any other time in the life of a dog is good for it, though starch in moderation is an excellent thing, more especially in winter, as it is a heating food and a fat producer.

It is notorious that certain strains of Bulldogs are particularly prone to eczema, and this is generally due to one of two reasons, and usually the latter—inbreeding, or a starchy diet persisted in for generation after generation ; and it may be stated here that the best way to treat a dog suffering from this disease of the skin is to commence by putting him on an absolutely non starchy diet, that is to say, by feeding him entirely on lean meat.

But for the dog in ordinary health a diet composed of a certain proportion of starch and albumen (meat) is the most beneficial. What the exact proportions should be must depend largely on the season of the year and on the animal itself, it being borne in mind that a greater quantity of starch may be given to the dog during cold weather than in hot.

For stock that is kept entirely for breeding, *i.e.*, stud dogs and brood bitches, meat should at all times form the bulk of the diet.

On this subject "Great Dane," in his "Principles of Dog Breeding," says: "Nitrogenous foods (meat, bones, milk, etc.) are absolutely necessary for the production of offspring, to build up growing dogs, and to repair the daily waste of tissue in mature animals, so that the proper development of all dogs depends largely on the nitrogen-suppliers constituting a considerable part of the ration."

Starch produces fat, and fat stock will not breed; or, in the case of brood bitches that are kept too fat, if they do breed, which is unusual, the dangers of whelping are greatly intensified. As the dog digests its food only once in twenty-four hours, one good meal a day is generally considered sufficient, and this should be given at about five or six o'clock in the afternoon, but what-ever the time decided upon, it should be adhered to, and the dog fed regularly at that hour.

An early morning meal of a light description is, however, to be recommended, more especially in cold weather, as a dog that has not broken its fast feels the cold far more than one that is fed both night and morning.

The early morning meal may consist of one or another of the patent foods, of which there are several excellent examples on the market, such foods as Rodnim (No. 2 grade), prepared by Messrs. Spratts Patents, Limited; Carta Carna, a hound meal that has stood high in public favour for many years; the Aylesbury Food, an excellent and nutritious mixture of starch and albumen; Dactyla, manufactured by Messrs. Rackham, of Norwich, and which, in addition to starch and albumen, con-tains a quantity of dried fruits, which have a beneficial and salutary effect, as they exercise a tonic influence on the system, which they keep in a cool and healthy condition. This is a food that may be particularly recommended for use in the spring and summer, and, with the others before named, for an occasional change in the winter.

For the early morning meal, therefore, one of the above-named foods should be given after prolonged soaking in boiling water. The food is easily prepared by putting it into a basin, covering with boiling water, stirring once or twice, and then covering the basin over, and setting it aside for an hour. No more should be made at a time than the dog can comfortably dispose of at one meal.

In the summer months a good biscuit, such as the world-

"WOODCOTE SMOKE."

The property of
DR. WALLACE AND H. W. WOODROFFE, ESQ.,
SKEGNESS.

"IVEL DAEDALUS."

The property of
    W. A. MURRAY, ESQ.,
    23, AVENUE ROAD, REGENT'S PARK,
    LONDON, N.

From the painting by Miss Monica Gray.

famed Spratts' dog cake, can be given instead of the hot meal, and the same biscuit should be used throughout the winter, for not only is it nourishing, containing as it does a certain percentage of desiccated meat, but it has a beneficial effect on the teeth and digestion by reason of the saliva producing-effect of masticating a hard biscuit. These biscuits can also be broken up and given soaked in gravy or even hot water.

So much, then, for the early morning meal or breakfast. The dinner or staple meal of the day requires more lengthy consideration.

Variety is, we hear, charming, and if so to the human being, it is equally so to the dog. A dog that receives exactly the same food week in and week out is never so ready for his meals, nor does he derive such benefit from his food as does one who receives a welcome change.

The following combinations form excellent meals, and most good results when the changes are rung as often as possible :—

Selected butchers' pieces, free from fat and small bones, stewed, the boiling gravy poured over one of the hound meals mentioned above, and allowed to stand for an hour ; the meat then cut up and added to the dish and mixed well in.

Or, in place of the hound meal, rice, well boiled with the meat ; though, as this is an excessively starchy food, it should be used only sparingly during the winter months, and given to breeding stock with great caution.

In place of rice, beans, which are eminently more nourishing and better in every way, though not all dogs will eat them. Cleaned and trimmed paunches, boiled and cut up and added to the hound meal as directed above.

In the spring, green paunches—those taken from grass-fed animals—can be given with great advantage, as they have a cleansing and beneficial effect on the skin and blood, raw and uncleaned, cut up into easily-swallowed pieces.

Sheep's head, well boiled, from which all the bones—and they are many—have been removed. This is especially nourishing for dogs in poor health, or for puppies, whelping bitches, etc.

Bullock's heads, boiled with hound meal soaked in the gravy.

Horseflesh is not to be recommended unless the purchaser is assured that it is not cut from the carcase of a diseased animal, and in the ordinary course may be left entirely out of the dog-owner's calculations.

Fish heads and pieces generally stewed down until all the bones are quite soft, the gravy mixed with brown bread (stale) or rice. If the bones are not quite soft through boiling, they must

E

be most carefully removed. At all times, and more especially in the spring of the year, green vegetables may be added to the dog's rations.

Fish bones, and the small brittle bones from game fowl, rabbits, hares, etc., should never on any account be given to dogs, as in many cases the giving of such bones has been attended by fatal results, due to the fact that the splintered and needle-sharp fragments pierce the bowels and cause death with great suffering.

The foregoing suggestions apply only to adult dogs of one year and more of age. Young puppies require feeding at more constant intervals, commencing with some six meals a day when they first leave the dam, and being gradually reduced to three at six months and two at twelve months of age.

At six weeks old, nourishing and easily-digested foods, such as the patent food manufactured by Messrs. Mellin, should be used. This food might well form the first and last meal of the day, the former given as early in the morning as possible, and the latter as late as possible at night. The Company's directions as to making should be carried out. The second meal may consist of some Spratts' Puppy Biscuit broken up. The third of some raw and lean meat passed through a mincing machine, or finely cut up with a knife. The fourth of some well-boiled oatmeal, with milk and a little sugar, or some good puppy meal mixed with boiling water or broth, and allowed to stand for an hour. The fifth meal may be the same, with the addition of a very little meat—sheep's head, or cleaned paunch well cut up.

Too much food should never be given at a time ; the maxim for breeders to remember in puppy feeding is "Little and often." If food is left on the dishes, it should be promptly taken away directly it is seen that the puppies have no appetite for it. Clean water should always be within reach of the dogs, but puppies may be given milk to drink with advantage ; either cows milk or condensed milk, mixed with warm water in the winter, or allowed to stand until cold in the summer.

In the case of adult dogs, the main meal of the day should be given after exercise, and the first meal or breakfast before exercise, and as early as possible in the day.

Exercise.—There is an idea prevalent that Bulldogs require less exercise than other breeds of dogs. Nothing could be more erroneous. A Bulldog requires fully as much exercise as any dog ; a greyhound perhaps excepted. Steady and regular exercise is absolutely necessary for his well-being, and he should be taken out at least once every day for a good constitutional,

"BULLET PROOF."

The property of

H. N. T. JENNER, ESQ.,
18, RANELAGH VILLAS,
HOVE.

Photo by H. St. John Cooper.

unless the dog-owner is lucky enough to own a large paddock, in which his dogs may be turned loose, when they will exercise themselves.

To suppose that exercise causes a Bulldog to run up " on the leg " is entirely wrong ; the more running about he gets the better he is constitutionally, and above all things a dog should be sound in limb and wind, or he is unworthy the name of Bulldog.

Young puppies at a very early age—from seven to eight weeks—should be accustomed to collar and lead, and taken out for walks in the public streets ; this will accustom them to the traffic. After a little while the lead may be taken off and the puppy allowed to run free, but he should always be kept under thorough control, and if he refuses to obey the order to come to heel, the lead must be again attached, and this system persisted in until the youngster thoroughly understands what is expected of him. The dog-owner should possess a whip, but should never use it except under exceptional circumstances. The continual thrashing of a dog breaks his spirit, sours his nature, and cows him, besides which the constant use of a whip, beside being cruel, is unnecessary. The sound of the voice and the sight of the whip should be sufficient to curb the most unruly, and if it is not, the fault lies in the education and bringing up of the dog.

CHAPTER VI.

THE ideal Bulldog kennel is that which affords its inmate absolute protection from cold and damp, equal protection from heat, the greatest possible facilities for cleansing and disinfecting, and the maximum of comfort for the dog, with equal convenience for its owner.

There are on the market a vast number of kennels, some of which are good and some bad. There is no half-way between the two, for if a kennel is not good it is bad, and the aim of the beginner in dog-keeping should be to supply himself with kennels that leave nothing to be desired, and which, with care, will last him for many years.

In the first place, the kennel should contain ample ground and air space, it should not be too small, nor yet should it be too large.

Not more than two kennels should be under the same roof—that is to say, a long range of kennels under one roof is a great mistake, as it allows for the spread of disease, and if one of the compartments of such a range is affected so will the rest be. Kennels should therefore be single, or, at the utmost, of the double variety, and each building should be placed as far from its neighbour as the ground space will allow.

Kennels made of stout and well-seasoned wood are in every way preferable to those built of brick.

Particular attention must be paid to the roof of the kennel. It should be of sufficient size as to thoroughly overlap and project beyond the building on every side, it should be wet-resisting and heat-resisting, and, preferably, it should be so constructed that if necessary it can be easily removed so as to throw the interior of the kennel entirely open.

The roof should be composed of three layers, the first of wood,

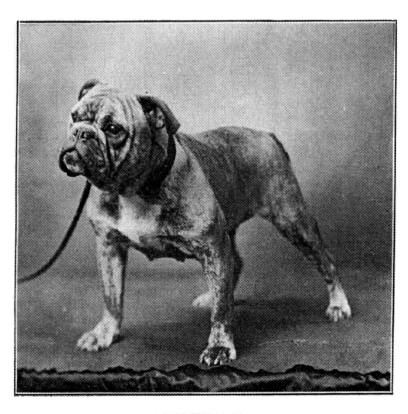

"TOTORA."

The property of

C. J. BRIDGLAND, ESQ.,

70, HIGH ROAD, BALHAM, S.W.

Photo by M. and F. Wykeham.

the second of roofing felt, and the third and outside layer of galvanised iron.

A roof composed only of wood is not moisture-proof, or, at any rate, if it is when it is first constructed, the warping and shrinking of the wood after it has been exposed to the weather for some time renders it thoroughly unsatisfactory for its purpose.

A roof composed only of iron is even more unsatisfactory. A kennel so roofed is too hot in summer, too cold in winter, and the moisture condensing on the under side of the iron renders the kennel damp. The walls should be of inch boards, tongued and grooved; the material should under no circumstances be less than seven-eighths of an inch thick. The outside walls should receive three (at least) coats of good oil paint, and an extra coat should be added in the autumn of each year as a further protection against the inclement weather of the coming winter. The inside walls may either be limewashed, or, what is better still, covered with a good sanitary distemper such as that manufactured by the Sanitas Company. This sanitary distemper lasts longer than the limewash, is cleaner, and does not come off on the hands and clothing of the attendant. It is also unnecessary to renew it so frequently as it would be if the walls were limewashed.

The flooring of the kennel, or, at any rate, the flooring to the sleeping compartment, must be of wood, not open battens, but a solid, jointed floor made in sections, so that it is easily removable. It may be made of the same material as the walls, but the wood used in its construction must not have a beaded edge. The crevices should be well filled in, so that there is no place in which dirt may lodge, and the boards of the floor should receive several coats of some light-coloured paint.

There are several designs of sleeping benches on the market, and these, as a rule, are satisfactory. It should be remembered, however, that it is better not to allow the dog to lay against the wall of the kennel for several reasons, one being that the wall is cold during the winter time, and another that the wall so soon becomes soiled.

A large and roomy box, with sides that are not too deep, is as good as anything for the dog to sleep in. Such a box may be obtained from the grocer's, that in which Quaker Oats is packed being a good size and shape for a medium or light-weight Bulldog, and as the cost of such boxes is very inconsiderable— fourpence being the usual price charged—they may be destroyed and used for firewood, and replaced by a new one about once in every month or six weeks.

Straw is, as a rule, the best bedding for dogs. The exceptional cases in which straw should not be used are for puppies of less than a fortnight old, and for dogs that make a practice of eating their bedding. In such cases hay, or clean, dry sacking, should replace the straw.

Wood shavings, especially those from pine, make an excellent and sanitary bed for the dog.

Whatever the bedding is composed of, too large a quantity should not be placed in the box or bench at one time, and every morning it should be taken out and burned, and fresh put in place of it. The box, or bench, should be in no way fixed inside the kennel, but should be so arranged that it may be easily taken out, washed, and placed in the sun or near a fire to dry.

A damp bed is as dangerous to the dog as it is to the human being.

The Kennel Yards.—Whenever circumstances permit, a yard should be formed with a concrete floor. On this the kennels may stand, and on this the dogs may exercise themselves during the day. And it should always be remembered, when constructing such a yard, and placing the kennels in position, that aspect is of the first importance, a southerly aspect being by far the best, failing that a westerly, but never a northerly or easterly.

When it is proposed to go in for breeding operations on a large scale, such a yard, or, rather, such a series of yards, is an absolute necessity. The concrete should be laid with a good "fall," or slope, which should decline to a properly trapped drain. No solid matter should, however, be allowed to pass down the drain, but should be taken up with a shovel and placed in a sanitary dustbin, which should be emptied at regular intervals.

It will be found that the use of sawdust greatly facilitates this operation. Ordinary fine sawdust from the sawmills may be used, but the sanitary sawdust that is to be bought commercially is the better for the purpose.

A sprinkling of sawdust should be made over the yard, and then swept up and put in the dustbin, and the yard afterwards swilled down with water to which some good disinfectant has been added.

It is false economy to be sparing in the use of disinfectant. Crude carbolic acid may be used in the outer yard, but for the interior of the kennels themselves some carefully prepared germicide, such as that made by the Sanitas Company—Jeyes' Fluid, or Izal—should always be used.

"CARTHUSIAN
WARRIOR."

The property of

J. C. MC COWAN, ESQ.,

HATFIELD, HERTS.

A rubber squeegee, such as is used by the street cleaners, is a most useful tool. This, a shovel, and a good competent broom, and a few pails, with some house flannels and drying cloths, should form the equipment of every well-kept kennel.

Though the floors of the kennels are made in sections, and easily removable, it is not, as a rule, necessary to remove them every day, though if the extra work involved in so doing is not objected to, it is the better plan. Every morning the floor should be cleaned out with sawdust, broom, and shovel, and a thin layer of fresh sawdust may be thrown down. Twice a week at least in the summer time the floors should be taken out and washed, and placed in the sun to dry, and in the winter time once a week. When possible it is better to dry the floors in the open air, but during the damp weather of winter the surface water should be well rubbed off with a flannel or cloth, and the sections put near, but not too close, to a fire or stove. If excessive heat is used in drying, the boards will soon shrink and warp, and the floor spoiled ; but, whatever be the drying process, it is imperative that both floors and sleeping benches must be thoroughly dried before returning them to the kennel.

If the slight extra cost is no object, it is by far the better plan to equip every kennel with a double set of floors and two sleeping benches, so that when one set of flooring and one sleeping bench is removed for cleaning, a fresh dry set can be immediately put in their place. The soiled set may then be cleaned at the kennelman's leisure, and returned to the kennel when another change is necessary. As the extra cost involved does not exceed a very few shillings, it is the plan to be most strongly recommended. It is impossible to breed and rear healthy puppies in dirty, insanitary, and damp kennels, and the owner who has the welfare of his dogs at heart will not begrudge the little necessary time and labour required for keeping the kennels always in spick-and-span order and "show condition."

The Disinfecting of Kennels.—This is a matter of the greatest, the most vital, importance, and is an operation that should be performed at regular intervals as a preventative against disease, and more particularly after any outbreak of disease such as distemper, mange, influenza, or other infectious complaints.

A dog should never, under any circumstances, be placed in a kennel in which a previous inmate has suffered from any illness unless the kennel has been most thoroughly disinfected in the interim. Some owners believe that the mere coating of the walls with limewash is a sufficient remedy for a disease-infected kennel, but limewash, though excellent in its way, is by no means

" MAHOMET."

The property of
    JAS. DUNCAN, ESQ.,
    4, BANK STREET,
    EDINBURGH.

Photo by Davis, Edinburgh.

a sufficiently powerful germicide to entirely destroy the germs of such diseases as distemper and mange, which seem to be particularly tenacious of life. Besides, it is practically impossible to invade every corner and crevice of a kennel with a brush dipped in limewash, and though to all appearances the walls may have been thoroughly covered, there is always some un noticed corner where the germs may live and thrive and continue their work of destruction. It is, as has been before stated, necessary that the kennel should lend itself to thorough disinfecting. Some of the designs put on the market by impractical makers seem to be arranged for the complete housing and sheltering of microbes, but even the recesses of these may be attacked if the owner knows how to set to work.

A thoroughly efficient method of disinfecting a kennel in which a dog suffering with an infectious disease has been housed, is as follows :—

First, clean out the kennel thoroughly, remove the floors, and if possible the roof. Then make a strong solution of " Creocide " (Sanitas Company), or Jeyes' Fluid, and with the aid of an efficient syringe, force the solution into every corner and crevice. This method of syringing is far preferable to the use of the brush, which has a habit of skipping over cracks and crevices. The germicide should be allowed to dry into the wood. It must not be forgotten that the floors and roof should be treated in the same way.

When the kennel is dry, floors and roof may be replaced. A sulphur candle, or the handy little " Sulphugators " made by the Sanitas Company, and sold in boxes of six for one shilling, should now be placed on a tin tray inside the kennel and lighted. Doors, windows, and ventilators are closed, and all cracks pasted over with paper to prevent the escape of the sulphurous smoke. The kennel should be left thus hermetically sealed for at least twenty-four hours, after which time the doors may be opened to allow the escape of the smoke, and the entire interior of the kennel treated to a good coating of limewash, or, better still, sanitary distemper. To thoroughly complete the work of disinfecting, the outside walls of the kennel should be syringed with the " Creocide " or Jeyes' Fluid, and afterwards treated to a coat of paint. A kennel so disinfected will be entirely free from disease germs, and a dog may be placed therein in perfect safety. The surrounding walls and concrete floor of the yard should also be treated with a strong solution of germicide, applied in the case of the walls with the syringe. All old straw, boxes, and in

fact everything that is not of value, should be burned, and in this
way the disease may be entirely stamped out.

FIG. 1.

The kennels which illustrate this chapter are reproduced by the
courtesy of the well-known firm of Messrs. Boulton & Paul,
of Norwich, from whose catalogue they are taken. The fact that
they are made by this firm is a sufficient guarantee of the
workmanship and of material used in their construction. The
designs are particularly well-suited to the requirements of the
Bulldog owner, and in particular would the writer call attention
to the double kennel with the passage at back (Fig. 1) from which
doors open into each kennel and run. The passage, while adding

BOULTON & PAUL. LTD   OCT. 1901.

FIG. 2.

considerably to the convenience of the owner or kennelman, also adds to the warmth and comfort of the sleeping berth for the dogs. This is an admirable kennel for whelping bitches. A feature in this kennel is the flap to the yards, which when raised as shown facilitates cleaning.

Figure 2 is a useful kennel under a span roof, it has a large covered run, which allows the dog plenty of freedom. The lower part of the run is covered with iron, which shields the inmates from draught and wet.

FIG. 3.

Figures 3 and 4, is a kennel designed by the writer and manufactured by Messrs. Boulton & Paul ; it is intended expressly for the dog owner who has not too much space at his disposal. Saving of space is effected by abolishing the division that usually separates the sleeping compartment from the outer run. During the daytime the shutter covering the bars is raised, and thus the entire kennel is turned into a day kennel; at night the shutter is closed, and the dog can sleep in comfort, free from draughts. One feature of this kennel to which the writer would call special attention is the roof; it is so constructed that it can be immediately entirely raised without the necessity for taking out screws or undoing nuts and bolts. This raising of the roof allows the interior of the kennel to be more thoroughly cleansed and disinfected than would otherwise be possible. During the hot weather the front part of the roof can be raised several inches, and fixed in place by means of the iron racks on either side, so that the maximum of ventilation without draught is afforded the inmates. This is particularly valuable in the case of a bitch with very young puppies, as instead of raising the shutter that covers the bars, the shutter can be kept fastened and the roof raised, with the result that the bitch is not annoyed or disturbed by other dogs or passing people. Even when raised to the highest point that the rack allows, the roof effectively protects the interior of the kennel from rain and from the direct rays of the sun. The floors of the kennel are of wood, made in sections and easily removable, as the writer always recommends. Cheapness, consistent with good material and good workmanship, is also a feature of this kennel, which is listed by the makers at £5.

CHAPTER VII.

SOME DISEASES OF DOGS.

It is impossible to deal at length with the many diseases which unfortunately canine flesh is heir to, in the restricted space which is now at the writer's disposal, and he cordially recommends those who wish to study this subject as they should, to expend a shilling in the purchase of " Dalziel's Diseases of Dogs," published by Messrs. Upcott, Gill & Co., of Drury Lane, London. Though the writer never recommends amateur doctoring, believing that the man who has made medicine his life-study is better able to prescribe for a patient, either human or canine, than the mere dabbler in science, he is nevertheless strongly of opinion that the dog owner should not be content to remain in absolute ignorance of matters that may at any time demand his attention, and should be able to afford a little timely help that may be the means of saving his dumb friend from considerable suffering.

In most cases the assistance of the owner should rather be of the nature of "first aid," and when the illness is such that the dog is seriously indisposed, the assistance of a qualified practitioner should be obtained without delay.

Distemper.—Of all diseases which are regarded by the dog owner in detestation and fear, and which commit the greatest ravage among the canine population, distemper stands first and foremost, most difficult to combat with, and most responsible for fatal issue. At one time in the history of the English dog distemper was unknown, and it is practically certain that it was introduced into this country from France, at about the end of the seventeenth century. Before that period no English writer on canine matters referred to the disease, but it is known to have existed in France long before that period ; so we may take it that we have to thank our French neighbours for the introduction into this country of a disease that is the bane and curse of the present-day dog owner's life.

"CRUMPSALL PYRAMID."

The property of
A. W. VOWLES, ESQ.,
GLEN VILLA, PELHAM PLACE,
CRUMPSALL, MANCHESTER

Photo by H. M. Benoliel, Esq.

F

Despite the efforts that have been made to stamp out the disease, the medical supervision of the dog shows, and the increased knowledge of dog owners, it yet seems to continue its destructive course unchecked. It is infectious and contagious in the highest degree, and the admittance into a kennel of a dog suffering from it will assuredly mean that nine-tenths of the kennel inmates, particularly puppies and dogs under two or three years of age, will in a very short space of time be down with the dreaded complaint. If, too, an infected dog escapes — as fortunately he rarely does—the lynx eyes of the veterinary inspector, and is allowed to enter a dog show, the disease spreads with lightning-like rapidity, and is carried home to kennels in every part of the country by animals that have come into contact with the infected specimen.

Fortunately, however, dog shows are not now, as once they were, the hotbeds of disease ; the Kennel Club's rules on the subject of veterinary examination are so stringent, and veterinary inspectors are so keenly on the look-out for distemper symptoms, that it may with safety be stated that not one infected dog in a thousand is allowed to pass into a show.

Some unscrupulous owners, however, occasionally send an animal to a show that does not happen to be infected with the disease himself, but, coming from an infected kennel, carries the disease with him, and infects other dogs with it. Clearly it is impossible for show authorities or veterinary inspectors to guard against this, but whenever absolute proof of such conduct on the part of an owner is to be obtained, it is the duty of any dog lover to report the case to the canine legislative body, the Kennel Club, and endeavour to secure for the offender that punishment which he so richly deserves.

, There are several forms of distemper—distemper of the head, distemper of the bowels, and simple distemper. In all forms the symptoms are much the same, and the most unmistakable symptom is the rapid wasting away of the dog. In three days a healthy, well-nourished animal becomes a mere bag of skin and bone. His eyes lack lustre, his smell is offensive—the distemper smell once known is never forgotten, nor mistaken for anything else. In cases of distemper of the head, a thick discharge comes from the nose and eyes, and usually there is a short, husky cough. The dog usually refuses his food, and mopes shivering in a corner, betraying by every action that it is seriously ill.

Unfortunately there is no cure for distemper. Many attempts have been made by scientists to find an anti-toxin, but all efforts have proved fruitless. The utmost that can be done for the

"SPA VICTORIA."

"SPA COUNTRY GIRL."

The property of
W. J. PLUM, ESQ.,
ST. NEOTS, HANTS.

patient is to keep it warm, free from draughts and cold, nourished, and if the action of the heart proves weak, stimulated.   Careful nursing, and nursing alone, is the only thing that can bring a patient through.

First and foremost the dog must be isolated, or the disease will instantly spread throughout the kennel.   In the chapter on kenneling, the writer advocated the use of single, or at the utmost double, kennels for the dogs, and the reason for that advice should now be apparent, for when dogs are all kennelled under one roof, the spread of such a disease as distemper is immediate, and cannot be coped with.

Sanitation must be practised rigorously.   All bedding coming from the infected kennel must be burned, all utensils used should be kept exclusively for the infected patient, and, when possible, the attendant who looks after the patient should not be allowed to come into contact with the uninfected dogs, or if he must, he must thoroughly disinfect his clothing, hands, and in particular his boots.

An outbreak of distemper during the summer-time is usually more far-reaching and destructive than one in the winter, and this is due to the swarms of flies that seem always to find a particular attraction in disease; these pests, passing from the infected kennels to the uninfected, spread the disease, and so the first care must be taken to exclude them, not only to check the spread of disease, but to save the sick animals from the irritation caused by presence of these insects.

The writer, unfortunately for himself, has had some considerable experience in distemper, and in a recent very severe summer outbreak of the disease, while casting about for some means to keep the flies at bay, he discovered a means of so doing that not only proved entirely efficacious, but which also proved of the greatest possible benefit to the patients, so much so that he is strongly of opinion that he owes the lives of some six or eight young dogs to the experiment.

The experiment consisted of obtaining from the nearest chemist a bottle of "Cresolene," and a small fumigating lamp; both lamp and liquid are placed on the English market by the well-known firm of Messrs. Allen & Hanbury, who recommend the fumigation of "Cresolene" for cases of cold, bronchitis, whooping-cough, and similar childish ailments.   The little pan of the stove was filled with the "Cresolene" fluid, and the stove lighted and placed for safety inside an old packing case, the front of which was left open, but protected with wire-netting.   Box and stove was then placed inside the kennel, and within a very few minutes, as soon, in fact, as the liquid began to give off vapour, the flies took a hurried departure. In a little while it was noticed that the dogs began to experience considerable relief from the germicide-laden air, their breathing became easier, and several, as though realising the beneficial effects they were obtaining, left their beds and clustered round the box, and there—after the replacing of the box in the kennel, was the signal for those who were able to leave their beds and make towards it.

The use of the Vapo Cresolene in the infected kennels, therefore, not only expelled the flies, and so prevented the spread of the disease, but, by disinfecting the air, attacked the distemper germs themselves in the most direct manner.

Since experimenting with this valuable remedy the writer has been in communication with Messrs. Allen & Hanbury, who have themselves communicated with the American owners of the patent, and the result is that a stove especially suitable for disinfecting kennels and hen houses, together with a liquid Cresolene in a cheaper form, is being put on the market especially for the use of dog owners and poultry keepers, as the remedy is as efficacious in a case of "gapes" in fowls as it is for distemper.

TREATMENT.—When an animal is attacked with what is unmistakably a case of distemper, he should, as before advised, be removed as far as possible from the neighbourhood of other dogs. The kennel or chamber in which the patient is placed should be airy, but perfectly free from draughts. If the time is winter, some means should be adopted for heating it artificially, and as this is almost impossible in a kennel unless an oil-stove is used, and the air consequently vitiated to the detriment of the dog, a dry and comfortable outhouse, loose box, or some similar structure should be utilised if it is not possible to take the animal into the house. An open fireplace is the best method of heating any room, for not only is it better as a heat-giver, but a burning fire in an open stove is the best possible method of ventilating a room.

The dog itself should at once be put into a flannel coat. This is easily made out of a piece of flannel, double thickness. It is cut to an oblong shape, two holes are made, through which the forelegs of the animal are passed, the front is drawn up loosely by means of a tape, and fastened round the dog's neck, and the two edges are sewed together over the animal's back ; this forms an efficient protection for the chest and lungs.

The bed may be as usual of straw or hay, and the boards of the floor outside the bed should be covered with a good thick

"ANDREW PRAZE."

The property of

MRS. JEMMETT BROWNE,
50, ASHBURNHAM MANSIONS,
CHELSEA.

Photo by Harrison.

layer of sanitary sawdust, or ordinary sawdust in which some Sanitas Powder has been sprinkled. The interior of the room or kennel should not be too strongly lighted, as the eyes are often affected by the disease, but entire darkness is not to be recommended. There are several medicines on the market, the makers of which all claim them to be infallible remedies for distemper ; and though some of these preparations are extremely valuable for the tonic effect they have on the system, which assists the dog to throw off the disease, it may be stated at once that there is no infallible cure for distemper !

Among the several distemper medicines that the writer has used, the distemper capsules made by Messrs. Wilson, of Ashford, Middlesex, have proved to be of undoubted assistance. In one case an attack of distemper was actually warded off by the timely use of this remedy; but when the disease has obtained a firm grip on the victim, the capsules can be used with advantage for the tonic effect they have on the system. Another excellent remedy to which equally high praise can be given is Dysto, manufactured by Messrs. Chambers, of Arnold, Notts, while a third remedy that has found high favour among dog owners for many years past is the excellent mixture made by Messrs. Benbows. Most particularly is this mixture valuable in restoring tone to the system after an attack of distemper, and it may be given with great success to all show-going dogs, as it strengthens the constitution and guards them against the risk of infection. It is also a useful tonic under ordinary circumstances, and keeps the system in a clean and healthy condition. A system of spring cleaning with the aid of Benbow's mixture is to be strongly recommended.

It will be soon found in ninety-nine cases out of a hundred that the distemper-stricken animal turns against his food. For a little while he may perhaps be tempted by his favourite fare, milk, to which a little Plasmon has been added, or broth should take the place of all other liquid ; a little selected lean and raw meat cut up into small pieces will often tempt a dog when all cooked foods fail, and if he can be persuaded to eat this there is nothing better for him.

When, however, the dog refuses to eat entirely, as unfortunately is usually the case, there is nothing for it but to feed him against his inclination with some good nourishing broth, beef or mutton, or that made from sheep's heads. Sometimes, however, the stomach is in such a weak state that it is unable to retain even this, and then the dog owner is obliged to fall back upon what is perhaps one of the most valuable forms of nourishment that has ever been introduced commercially. Liquid Kreochyle is a meat extract in a liquid and highly concentrated form, but so prepared that it is retained by the stomach, no matter in what a debilitated and weakened condition it may be. It is nourishment in its highest and best form, being pure albumen in a liquid state. No preparation is necessary, no admixture of water; the food can be poured straight from the bottle down the dog's throat, or can be given by means of a drencher or teaspoon. A few doses of this food will generally bring back the dog's appetite to a certain degree; but if the effect is not immediate, the dog can be entirely fed on the Kreochyle, with no other form of nourishment for many days if necessary. Warmth, pure air, sanitation, and nourishment, are therefore the only possible things to provide in a case of distemper.

When the action of the heart is weak, and the dog seems to be sinking, the giving of a little stimulant, such as weak brandy and water, is to be advised, or a few drops of brandy may be mixed with a teaspoonful of the Kreochyle.

The dosing of distemper-stricken dogs with all sorts of medicines and remedies is to be strongly discountenanced, for the stomach, already in a weakened and irritated condition, is further harassed by the introduction of these entirely useless mixtures. The veterinary surgeon who, when called in to a case of distemper, sends a huge bottle of evil-smelling mixture, with directions to be administered every two or three hours, may possibly be a clever man in other branches of the profession, but he is the man for the dog owner to avoid

Eczema.—As has been before stated, many dogs are predisposed to this skin complaint from one of three causes—inbreeding, and its consequent impoverishing of the blood and lowering of the animal's vitality; or a wrong system of feeding, indulged in possibly for several generations; and lastly, the presence of worms in the bowels.

When eczema makes its appearance, the treatment should consist of first cleansing the system, which is best done by prescribing a good dose of liquorice powder. Epsom salts is sometimes given, but the writer is of opinion that Epsom salts has done far more harm than it has ever done good, and is not a fit medicine to throw even to the dogs. Liquorice powder is excellent for this purpose, and should be used in preference.

The diet should receive next and immediate attention. Starchy food in any form should, at any rate, temporarily, be dispensed with, and the animal fed practically entirely on meat—

"KILBURN PROFESSOR."

The property of
STANLEY B. JONES, ESQ.,
MACKWORTH HOTEL, SWANSEA.

lean meat, raw or cooked.   Finally, the skin should be dressed with a soothing ointment.   Sulphur ointment is very good for the purpose, and may be made by mixing flowers of sulphur with vaseline ; but a far better remedy than this is the Eczoline Ointment that was introduced some years back by Mr. W. W. Hunter, of Swindon, Wilts.   This ointment immediately allays all itching, and quickly puts the skin into a normal, healthy, and clean condition.   It may also be used with as much success in cases of mange as in cases of eczema.

It must be remembered that outward applications in case of eczema are not likely to produce so immediate and beneficial an effect than as when they are assisted by judicious and moderate dosing and a careful regard to the animal's diet. Eczema is practically the outward and visible sign of an inward derangement, and the attack must be directed to the seat of the trouble.

Eczema is not infectious, and is not passed from dog to dog, though, as when, as is often the case, a bad and injudicious system of feeding is in vogue, many animals belonging to the same kennel will be attacked by the disease almost simultaneously, and this leads dog owners to believe that, like mange, eczema is contracted by one dog through coming into contact with another.

Diet is of the utmost importance, and it is only by careful dieting, long persisted in, that an animal may be entirely freed from this complaint.   Starch should be reduced to a minimum. Green vegetables should be given, and while the disease is at its worst the diet should consist entirely of lean meat and green vegetables.   The green paunches, before referred to in the chapter on feeding, are invaluable in cases of eczema, as they exercise a very cleansing effect on the system.

Eczema may often be confounded by the novice with mange, and though to the unpractised eye there is much similarity between the diseases, they are in reality of entirely different origin, and require different treatment.

Mange is produced by a mite, so small as to be invisible to the naked eye.   It is propagated by eggs, and transmitted from dog to dog by direct or indirect contact.   Thus, while eczema is decidedly not a contagious disease, mange most certainly is.

The mite burrows under the skin, discharging a poisonous fluid, which causes intense irritation ; the skin becomes inflamed, and, to a certain degree, enlarged or swollen ; it is then broken, pustules appear, which discharge freely, the hair falls off, scabs make their appearance, and, if the disease is allowed to go on unchecked, the animal's entire body becomes involved. In this, mange differs from eczema, as the latter is generally entirely local, only certain portions of the body being attacked, while the rest is entirely free from the disease.

As mange is caused by a germ, the natural and proper treatment of it is by means of a germicide. The destruction of the germs that cause the mischief is the object to be aimed at by the dog owner, and for this purpose he may use any really reliable germicide on the market. Eczoline, before referred to, is a most excellent remedy, and it has the advantage of being equally efficacious both in cases of eczema and mange; therefore the novice who is unable to distinguish between the two may use this preparation with the certainty that he is doing right.

The use of a germicide in the case of eczema would be as futile as inward dosing in the case of mange, so the owner should early make himself acquainted with the appearance of the diseases, in order that he may be better able to cope with them should the necessity arise.

While water should not be allowed to touch the coat of a dog suffering from eczema, a thorough good washing, using a soap containing a germicide, is of the first necessity in case of mange. He must then be thoroughly dried, and, for safety, the towel or cloth which has been used for this purpose should be burned. Such methods as these, though apparently extravagant to the thrifty soul, are, in reality, time and money saving in the end.

Most kennelmen have their own pet mange dressing, by which they are prepared to swear, and which they declare are infallible. In ninety-nine cases out of a hundred this dressing consists of black sulphur, oil of tar, paraffin, and a little olive oil. Some use more of one ingredient and less of another, some use the paraffin and sulphur alone, and so the changes are rung, but the basis of all home-made dressing is much the same. An animal so treated is in an extremely messy and unpleasant condition, but, as the disease must be conquered at any cost, the temporary discomfort of the dog, and the almost equal discomfort of the owner, cannot be taken into account. Still, when a thoroughly efficacious dressing is to be obtained that is cleanly in use and unattended by horrible smells, the dog owner will be wise to avail himself of it, and such a dressing is Eczoline. As mange produces a general overheating of the system, the use of a gentle aperient, such as liquorice powder, is to be advised.

"BUDDUG."

The property of
    MRS. W. W. CROCKER.

The diet should be light, and for some few days rather inclined to be of a sloppy nature.

The first thought of the owner who has an infected dog must be to isolate him from the other dogs. On no account should other dogs be allowed to come into direct contact with him, for the disease is contagious in the highest degree. All bedding taken from the infected kennel should be immediately burned. Germicides should be used with a liberal hand, and the attendant must see to it that his hands are disinfected before he attempts to handle an unaffected dog.

After the disease has been cured, the kennel should be subjected to the most rigorous cleansing, and disinfected in the manner described in the previous chapter.

Worms are the great pests of dog life, and it may safely be assumed that every dog that has not been treated with a vermifuge is affected. Fortunately for the dog owner, there is on the market at the present time a great number of safe and reliable vermifuges, any of which may take the place of the once generally used areca nut and santonine, or the more primitive powdered glass, turpentine, tobacco, calomel, and other abominations.

Worms found in the dog are of two distinct kinds, round and tape. The former are, generally, after the use of a good vermifuge, expelled in clusters, or bunches, and have somewhat the appearance of short lengths of yellowish-white cotton or very coarse hair. The latter resemble the article from which they take their name, and sometimes attain an enormous growth; in fact, several feet in length. Usually the tape worm is expelled in segments, though sometimes, after the use of an effective vermifuge, the entire length may be evacuated by the dog.

At one time the treatment of tape worm and round worm differed, areca nut and santonine being given to effect a cure of the latter and male fern extract of the former. Nowadays the several excellent vermifuges which the writer has used are as efficacious in the case of one as the other.

Those who wish to compound their own vermifuge, and who have a conservative leaning towards areca nut, should purchase the nut in its whole state, not ground up as many chemists sell it. The work of grinding the nut is a very laborious and protracted occupation, but it must be persisted in if the best results are to be attained. The dose is one grain for every pound that the dog weighs, but no more than two drachms should be given at the utmost. The areca nut powder may be administered mixed in fat, treacle, or some such substance, but the administering of the dose is at the best an unpleasant and dirty performance, which may be rendered a degree less unpleasant if the areca nut mixture is first wrapped in a small piece of tissue paper.

When so many excellent vermifuges are obtainable at a very low cost, the preparation and administering of such a bulky dose as is necessary in the case of areca nut is scarcely to be recommended, and for the guidance of the beginner the writer appends a list of thoroughly reliable and useful vermifuges, all of which he has tried with the most satisfactory result.

Wilson's Worm Capsules (Wilson & Co., Ashford, Middlesex) are made in various sizes to suit the various breeds of dogs, from toy puppies or kittens to St. Bernards. They are handy in use, thoroughly efficacious, and require no after-dosing with castor oil. The effect is immediate, large quantities of worms being brought away within an hour at the utmost of administering the dose. No ill-effect to the dog's health results from the use of these capsules. To administer the capsule, which should be given, to achieve the best results, on an empty stomach, the capsule is held between the fore-finger and thumb of the right hand, the upper jaw of the dog is grasped with the left hand and the mouth forced open, the capsule is then pushed well to the back of the throat and forced down with the end of the fore-finger. A few drops of warm milk materially assist the solution of the outer gelatine covering of the capsule, but no quantity should be given immediately after the dose, nor is the administration of the hot milk or broth an absolute necessity. These capsules may be given to the dog at any age, but they are particularly suited to animals of six months and upwards.

The Ruby Remedy has been quite lately introduced, and for very young puppies is to be most highly recommended. It is prepared and sold by a dog owner and breeder of great experience, to wit, Mr. R. E. Nicholas, of Bitterne Park, Hants, who is known to fame as "Great Dane," the author of the invaluable handbook on breeding which has several times been referred to in this book. Ruby is a liquid of an oily nature, and of a colour to warrant its name. Puppies that have just left the dam may be dosed with it with perfect safety, and the results are uniformly excellent. No harm whatever results to the dog, and worms are immediately and entirely expelled from the system. The relieving of young puppies from these internal pests is a work of the first importance. Worm-infested puppies cannot possibly do well, and unless some steps are taken to rid them

"HIS NIBS."

The property of
    HUGH BROADBENT, ESQ.,
    5, WEST STREET,
    STALYBRIDGE.

of the pests they absolutely destroy the vitality and sap the very lives of the creatures in whom and on whom they live. The breeder must therefore take the earliest opportunity to rid his puppies of worms, but he must also assure himself that he is using a vermifuge that, while attacking the worms, will do no harm to their host. Such a vermifuge is Ruby.

The presence of worms in puppies or in adult dogs that have been in any way neglected may be taken for granted. Naturally they are present sometimes in a greater and sometimes in a lesser degree, but, in whatever numbers they may be, their presence is a menace to the health and to the very lives of the puppies.

Klensene.   Klensene Worm Powder, which is put up in capsules, is another thoroughly efficient vermifuge, quick and certain in its action, and one that, while attacking the pests, has no ill-effect whatever upon their host.

Castrique.   In Castrique we have a vermifuge of an entirely different nature to any of the foregoing ; in fact, it is distinctly different to any vermifuge on the market. While most vermifuges are quick in action, and produce immediate results—if they are efficacious—Castrique is a slow cure, but, though slow, it is most certain in the good work it performs. Castrique is a tonic remedy that performs a double service. It thoroughly cleanses and strengthens the stomach and intestinal canals, rendering them unfit abiding places for worms, and at the same time dissolves the worms themselves ; thus not only is the dog freed from the pests, but is strengthened and fortified against further attack. Castrique is sold in the form of a white powder, and also in capsule form. The writer recommends the use of the remedy as a powder, as in this way it is most easily administered to young puppies. The powder can be put into milk or sprinkled over the food, and is readily taken by the puppies, so that practically no dosing is required at all.   Its tonic effect is most marked, and the health of the puppies so treated improves visibly after the first two days.

When a puppy has been neglected, and is most badly infected, the use of a quick-acting remedy, such as Messrs. Wilson's Capsules or the Ruby, is to be recommended. After that should follow a course of Castrique, which quickly restores to the animal the health and vitality of which the worms it has harboured have robbed it.

But whatever may be the remedy selected, it cannot be too firmly impressed on the mind of the dog owner that, firstly, a remedy is absolutely necessary ; secondly, that in the very

"BOB UPANWYN,"

The property of

MRS. JEMMETT BROWNE,
50, ASHBURNHAM MANSIONS,
CHELSEA, S.W.

*From the Painting by
Arthur Kelsey.*

unlikely event of the dog or puppy not being infested with worms, the administration of such a vermifuge as one of these described can do no harm whatever ; and thirdly, the persistent use of a good vermifuge throughout the entire life of the dog, from puppyhood to mature age, and after. Worm-infested puppies seldom attain maturity. They are unthrifty, their food does not nourish them, they are extremely liable to disease, their breath is offensive, their coats hard and staring ; and lastly, the presence of worms in the dog, by lowering the system and impoverishing the blood, undoubtedly produces eczema.

CHAPTER VIII.

Champion "Prince Albert."—The property of Mr. Luke Crabtree, of Lea Grange, Blackley, near Manchester; is universally acknowledged to be one of, if not the best, stud and show Bulldogs living, which is fully proved by the consistent manner in which he reproduces his good qualities in all stock sired by him. "Prince Albert" is the winner of many hundreds of prizes, including championships at the best shows throughout the country. On the bench he has taken everything possible, having won over 400 first and special prizes, fifteen Championships, numerous cups, and has won the special for best dog in show of any breed over thirty times. He was sired by "Katapult," himself a son of the celebrated champion, "Boomerang." Bred by Mr. Murrell, "Prince Albert" has been for long in the possession of Mr. Crabtree, under whose ownership he has done all his winning. Valuable as he has proved himself to be as a show dog, it is perhaps as a sire that he will be longest remembered, for amongst others of the first magnitude of which he is the father are the sensational champion, "Broadlea Squire," "Queen o' Scots," "Yorkshire Relish," "Moston Consort," "Kumhardi Babi," "Prince of Darkness," "Probang," and other good ones too numerous to mention by name. "Prince Albert" is by "Katapult," ex "Dame Fortune," "Katapult" by champion "Boomerang," ex "First Attempt," "Dame Fortune" by "Preston Lion," ex "Lancashire Lass," she being twice bred to champion "Rustic King;" while, on the other side, "Prince Albert" inherits the famous "King Orry" blood.

"Moston Major."—This well-known dog, bred and owned by Mr. Luke Crabtree, has been, like the late illustrious champion, "Boomerang," a late dog to develop. He has a grandly shaped head, with small, well-carried ears, large underjaw, turn-up and lay-back, deep stop, and good cushion. He

"HIELAND DAME."

The property of
LIEUTENANT BAIRD,
WOODLEIGH,
CHELTENHAM.

Photo by Ovinius Davis,
Edinburgh.

has plenty of bone, with strong ribs, short back, and short down tail. He is winner of many prizes, including second, Edgworth; first and second, ten guinea bowl, and four other specials, Rushden; firsts at Sale, Chesterfield, Driffield, Norden, Upholland, Northwich, Wakefield, etc. He is a son of champion "Prince Albert," his dam "Moston Busy" being by "Dartaway," ex "Princess Orry," she by "King Orry," thus "Moston Major" is twice bred to this celebrated strain.

"**Moston Michael.**" Mr. Luke Crabtree's well-known kennels have been strengthened by the recent introduction of this fine dog. "Moston Michael" was bred by Mr. Fergusson, his sire being "Swashbuckler," a champion Bromley Crib dog, his dam being "Vesey Maud," she by "Catseye," ex "Bullring Blackberry," a Highwayman bred bitch. Of him the *Stock-keeper* has recently said : "He is the embodiment of all the essentials required in one of the breed, not exaggerated in anything, but a sound, high quality dog of 'the' type, which we think no fancier will contradict. In head he is as near perfection as it is possible to wish for. His lay-back, width, and turn-up of underjaw, long flat skull, and wrinkle will always carry him through. A compact-bodied dog, with a rare forearm and splendidly placed shoulders, and the soundest of movements imaginable." This high opinion of the dog is also shared by the critics on the staffs of *Our Dogs* and of the *Illustrated Kennel News*. He is a dark brindle in colour, with a white chest, and, though he has been but little shown, he has already a good number of prizes to his credit, won at some of the leading shows.

"**Prince of Darkness.**"—Owned by Mrs. May, of Sandhurst, Marine Drive, Rhyl, is a massive-headed brindle with a rare, grand, and typically finished face full of Bulldog character and expression. Well-placed, small and correctly carried ears, good-shaped skull, deep stop, while in lay-back and turn-up of underjaw there is nothing further to be desired. His body is short and compact and low to ground. At seven shows, commencing with Birkenhead, where he took third to his sire, champion "Prince Albert," he has taken thirty-seven prizes, including firsts and specials under Messrs. Rylance, Deacon, Ireland, and Crabtree ; also the London Bulldog Society's Novice Bowl, twice the British Bulldog Club twenty-five guinea Bulldog Cup and Novice Bowl, the "Broadlea Squire" and "Cheetham" twenty-five guinea challenge cups, gold commemoration medals, etc. He was whelped in January, 1903, being bred by his present owner. He is a son of champion

" Prince Albert" by " Baby She," she by " Fighting Buller," ex " Gypsy Blaze," a " Chatley Nob " and " Dockleaf" bred bitch.

"**Mersey King.**"—The property of Mr. James Woodbridge. Sire "Prince Albert," dam " Lady Felto " by champion " Kater-felto." Born 7th February, 1903 ; colour, brindle ; weight, forty-eight pounds ; bred by the owner ; winner of over fifty prizes, including cups and specials. His first appearance was at Bristol Show, November, 1903, when nine months old, where he won two seconds, one third, and a fourth prize. At Blackpool Show, January, 1904, he went through his classes from open to puppy, winning five firsts and six specials. At Manchester Show, March, 1904, he won a first, two seconds, and thirteen specials, including the " Broadlea Squire" Challenge Cup, the Novice Cup for best dog bred by exhibitor. He has won under sixteen different judges. *Our Dogs*, January 16th, 1904, said : " Mersey King" came out on top, although under twelve months old. He is well-developed, having a broad, flat skull, good lay-back, under-jaw, and turn-up ; he is a good length from eye to ears, which are small and well-carried, wide in front, and good placement of shoulders and nice spring of rib ; he is nicely cut in loin, and shows a roach back." *The Field* says : " ' Mersey King ' is one of our best dogs. He is a stock-getter, and, like his illustrious sire, passes on his good qualities to his progeny."

"**St. Amant.**"—The property of Dr. T. P. Grosart Wells, of St. Albans. A dark brindle dog ; born March 27th, 1903 ; sire "Moston Boxer" (by champion " Prince Albert," ex " Brown Bread ") ; dam "Speculation" (by " Balaclava," ex "Down-genie ") ; weight, forty-four pounds ; phenomenal head properties ; circumference of skull, nineteen and a half inches ; immense underjaw, chop, and wrinkle ; eyes wide apart ; thin rose ears set on in the right place. In competition, Mr. J. H. Taylor judging, "St. Amant" took the special prize for best-headed Bulldog in the show, beating champion " Heath Baronet" and other notable winners. Another specialist judge writes of this dog : "I consider ' St. Amant ' the best-headed dog I ever saw in my life ; his head is an absolute study of perfection."

Champion "Nuthurst Doctor."—This deservedly suc-cessful and well-known dog was sired by champion "Ivel Doctor," his dam being champion " Primula." He was bred by Mr. E. A. Vicary, and has been owned from puppyhood by his present mistress, Mrs. Edgar Waterlow, of 64, Compayne Gardens, West Hampstead. "Nuthurst Doctor" is a dog possessing an immense and correctly shaped skull, a rare turn-up

"MERSHAM JINGO."

The property of
MRS. CARLO F. C. CLARKE,
RADNAGE FARM,
STOKENCHURCH, BUCKS.

Photo by H. St. John Cooper.

of underjaw, while in the true Bulldog expression and character he is excelled by no dog of the present day. A very short, compact dog, with great width of front, immense bone, and the neatest of tails, he has had a winning career since he was first shown in May, 1902, when he was first in the puppy class at the L.K.A. show at Richmond, first Cheetham Hill and London Bulldog Society, Royal Aquarium, Royal Bulldog Club Incorporated Show, and at Cruft's (1903); first in limited at Richmond, Cheetham Hill, Ealing, Kennel Club, London Bulldog Society's Show, Birmingham, Royal Aquarium, Wimbledon Bulldog Club Incorporated Show, Cruft's Metropolitan Canine Association's Show; first in open classes at the L.K.A. Show, Worthing, Sutton, Burton-on-Trent, Richmond, Buxton, Eastbourne, Sandy, Southampton, Streatham, and Bristol. He won his Championships at the L.K.A. Show, Southampton Show, and Bristol Show, 1904. In all he has won fifty-five firsts, fifty-six seconds and thirds, and 104 specials, among which are the British Bulldog Club's fifty guinea Challenge Vase, their twenty-five guinea Challenge Vase, the Bromley Crib, the Retlaw, the F. W. Taylor, the Colonel Mitchell, the Mrs. Tottie's ten guinea, the Berrie, the Hayes Redwar (three times and finally) challenge cups, and the following trophies : Dewar's Challenge Shield, Jeyes' Challenge Trophy, and other specials too numerous to mention. As a sire he is equally successful, and some of his progeny, which includes that sterling bitch, "Nuthurst Choice," show remarkable promise.

"**Corsham Bogie.**"—The property of Mr. and Mrs. W. Hugh Berners, of Inward, Sudbury, Suffolk. Though he has been an enthusiastic owner and breeder of Bulldogs for some thirty-five years, Mr. Berners has shown but rarely. Had he been eager for show honours, there is but little doubt that this good bitch, "Corsham Bogie," would have a vast number of prizes to her credit, and would in all probability have earned the prefix "champion" long before this. Of undoubted value though "Corsham Bogie" would have proved as a show bitch, she has proved herself, which is even more satisfactory to her owners, a brood bitch of the first magnitude. A dark brindle, she has marvellous quality all over, with a beautifully modelled skull, good chest, and set on of shoulder, and she is a thorough Bulldog in expression. The last litter by her was particularly successful, containing at least three dogs that will help to make Bulldog history, these three being " King Pluto," now owned by Mr. Hurdle, of Plymouth ; "Justice of Peace," who remains the property of his breeders ; and " Berners " (so named in honour of his breeder), now the property of that old-time fancier, Mr. G. W. Richards. These dogs were sired by "Kumhardi Babi" by champion "Prince Albert," their dam, "Corsham Bogie," being by "Graveney Robert," ex "Lady Monk," both being by "Stockwell," ex "Mrs. Quilp."

"**Justice of Peace**," who alone of the three dogs before referred to remains in his breeders' possession, is a grand young dog with a future before him, if his owners decide upon exhibiting him. A big one, with no end of bone, good ribs, and chest, roach back, and well-cut-up loin, he is very short in face, and has great breadth and width, nice length of skull, from eye to ear, and plenty of wrinkle. He has the true Bulldog expression and gait, and is as a Bulldog should be, as sound as a bell.

"**King Pluto**."—The property of Mr. A. Hurdle, of Seaton Avenue, Plymouth, litter brother of the foregoing. "King Pluto" is a black brindle, of about forty pounds weight. He is a grandson of champion "Prince Albert," being by "Kumhardi Babi," ex "Corsham Bogie," he is one of the low and cloddy sort, with great bone, good chest and middle piece, and perfect spring of rib; his skull, ears, wrinkle, temple, and fore-face are phenomenal, his cushion is wonderfully developed ; he also has a good turn-up of inner jaw. He was whelped in December, 1902, so he still has plenty of time to improve. He has only been shown on two or three occasions ; he won first novice, second limit, third junior, at the Bulldog Show, 1904. First and reserve for the best dog in show, any breed, at Liskeard ; he also won at Lynn and Sudbury. He has proved himself a good dog at stud. He was bred by Mrs. W. H. Berners, and is a litter brother to "Justice of Peace."

"**Berners**."—The last of the trio is owned by Mr. G. W. Richards, of Hever, in Kent, a grand young brindle of such quality as is very rarely seen ; possibly one of the reasons that induced Mr. Richards to purchase "Berners" at a big figure, was the strong resemblance that exists between this dog and the celebrated old champion "British Monarch," which Mr. Richards purchased some sixteen years ago, at the then record price of £125. "Berners" possesses a good square skull, short well-ribbed-up body, carried on four sound and well-boned legs. He stands naturally and well, and is a sound and active dog, and will in all probability work his way to the very top of the tree, as he is of the right type, and deserves the careful attention of all breeders who are bent on perpetuating it.

"**Crumpsall Pyramid**."—This young brindle dog, the property of Mr. A. W. Vowles, of Glen Villa, Crumpsall, near

"MERSHAM JUMBO."

The property of
  MRS. CARLO F. C. CLARKE,
  RADNAGE FARM,
  STOKENCHURCH, BUCKS.

Photo by H. St. John Cooper.

Manchester, is a dog of striking personality, possessing as he does all the much-desired points in a very marked degree. He has great width of front, with good short back, and well-rounded ribs. It is but natural that his body properties should be so strong, as he is twice bred to " Don Pedro," his sire being " Balaclava," who was litter brother to three champions, his dam, " Westbourne Lassie," being by " Hicks," ex " Hampshire Beauty," " Hicks " by " Don Salano," ex " Habnab.' " Pyramid " has a good, square, well-balanced head, the much to be desired big nose, while his turn-up of underjaw is remarkable. He was bred by Mr. F. Buckland, and now that he is in Mr. Vowles' possession, he is siring some stock that is already winning, and will be heard of later.

" **Kilburn Professor.**"—The property of Mr. Stanley Jones, Mackworth Hotel, Swansea ; is a low, cloddy, dark golden brindle, with a broad natural front, immense bone, good stop and turn-up, eyes wide apart, well-wrinkled broad skull, short face, plenty of loose skin. Vigorous and certain stock-getter. His breeding leaves nothing to be desired, a perfect combination of the best Bulldog blood ; his sire, " Pentemenon " is the sire of some of our best dogs at stud and on the bench to-day, whilst his dam, " Cypripedin," has already won two Championships. He is the winner of twenty-nine firsts, cups, specials, etc., at seven shows—London B.D.C., Redhill, Baldock, Yeovil, Swansea, Merthyr, and Streatham, always being in the money at every show exhibited. His latest wins are, two firsts, silver cup, and other prizes, Streatham, September 22nd, 1904. He is by " Pentemenon," ex " Cypripedin." " Pentemenon " by " Champion Boaz," ex " Mods." She by the " Kalifa," ex " Doddles."

" **Woodcote Smoke.**"—The property of Dr. S. Wallace and Mr. H. W. Woodroffe, Skegness, Lincolnshire. " Woodcote Smoke " contains the valuable " Rodney Stone " blood, his sire being " Buckstone," by champion " Rodney Stone," ex " Blackun ; " his dam " Lady Kitchener," by " Jack of Spades," ex " Daisy Bell." " Woodcote Smoke " is a young and very vigorous dog, whelped 3rd October, 1901, weighing about forty-eight pounds. A proved stock-getter. In colour he may be described as a dark brindle, shaded on fore and hind quarters and back with grey. He has an immense square skull, short face, and deep stop, well-turned underjaw, and small perfectly-carried rose ears. He possesses a typical pear-shaped body, with grandly sprung ribs, roach back, good cut-up of loin, light hind-quarters, short straight tail, set on low deep chest, and good shoulders. He excels in true Bulldog character, and from his pedigree should prove invaluable to breeders His sire is well known. His dam is one of the best-headed bitches living, and is litter sister to "Woodcote Sourface," the dam of "Woodcote Sweetface," one of Mr. W. J. Pegg's noted winners.

"**His Nibs.**"—The illustration of this dog given in the pages of this book is taken from a photograph made of him while he was still in his puppyhood, so that justice has scarcely been done him. He is a massively-boned golden brindle, with a very short back, and a proper old-fashioned roach. He has extraordinary width of underjaw, with fine upward sweep, a short screw tail, and light hind-quarters. His skull is large, well-wrinkled, and square, with good length from eye to ear. His ears are as near perfection as possible. This dog is bred on the lines of the old type. He is very sound, and is as hard as nails. He is by "Sundridge," ex "Strategy;" the former by "Pentemenon," ex "Lady Fulham;" "Strategy" by "Klondike," ex "Briarwood." He is the property of Mr. Hugh Broadbent, of 5, West Street, Staleybridge, under whose ownership he has won two firsts, special, and second at Hyde, second at Ashton, third and reserve Cheetham Hill.

"**Mahomet.**"—Undoubtedly this dog ranks among the best heavy-weight Bulldogs living. Indeed, many competent judges consider him without a compeer in the heavy brigade. His successes in the ring have been considerable, but are scarcely a criterion of his outstanding qualities, for although most of the leading dogs, including at least four champions, have had to give place to him, he has not been so far fortunate enough to secure the coveted card. He has been four times reserved for the position. A dog possessing such tremendous skull of the much desired length, such wide underjaw and lay-back, such massive bone and beautiful form throughout, must always find a place in the first rank. He is by "Khalifa," ex "Lady Dorothy," by "Rodney Stone." Among his principal winnings are two firsts, Edinburgh, 1903; second and third, Birmingham, 1903; first and second, Cruft's, 1904; three firsts, Bulldog Club (Incorporated) Show, 1904; two firsts, Edinburgh, 1904; also first at Newcastle, Glasgow, Greenock, etc., and winner of the British Bulldog Club's twenty-five guinea cup twice, the Thackeray soda cup, the Berrie cup, and ten guinea trophy, medals, etc. He is owned by J. Duncan, Esq., 4, Bank Street, Edinburgh.

"**Carthusian Warrior.**" — Is a massive brindle dog, possessing in a marked degree that upward sweep of underjaw, which is now unfortunately giving place only too often to an underjaw of the shelf or straight projecting type. If for no other

"MERSEY KING."

The property of
JAMES WOODBRIDGE, ESQ.,
39, LABURNUM ROAD,
FAIRFIELD, LIVERPOOL.

reason than that he is so strong in this feature, " Carthusian
Warrior" is a dog that should command the attention of all
breeders, but he has many other good points to recommend him
—immense bone, a strong and massive body, a good square
skull, and well broken-up face, with the right expression. He is
by " Carthusian Cerberus," ex " Mab," by " Wyley Monarch," and
weighs fifty-six pounds. He has won first at Oldham, first
Wallingford, and second at the Kennel Club Show. His owner
is Mr. J. C. McCowan, of Hatfield, Hertfordshire.

" Ivel Daedalus."—This is a massive white dog, bearing a
strong resemblance to the celebrated champion " Ivel Doctor," to
whom " Daedalus " is twice bred, he being by " Ivel Demonax,"
by champion " Donax," ex " Ivel Daffodil," by champion " Ivel
Doctor." His dam, " Ivel Dorothy," being by champion " Ivel
Doctor," ex " Ivel Dorry." Thus it will be seen he is full of the
valuable " Ivel " blood, which has produced such grand dogs
as champion " Nuthurst Doctor " and " Woodcote Lily."
" Daedalus " is the property of Mr. W. A. Murray, of 23,
Avenue Road, Regent's Park. He is the winner of very many
prizes, including first and second, London Bulldog Society ; two
firsts and four seconds, Wimbledon, 1902 ; first, Harpenden ;
two firsts, Middlesex Canine Society ; the London Bulldog
Society's ten guinea cup ; and gold medal for the best Bulldog
under eighteen months of age ; second and third at the L.K.A.
Show, 1902. During 1903 this dog was not shown at all, but in
1904 he recommenced his winning career by taking second and
third at Croydon, first and special at Sudbury, first and second at
Brighton, first and two seconds Cambridge, first Newport Pagnell,
second and special Crystal Palace Kennel Club Show, three
seconds Sandy. " Ivel Daedalus " is siring some puppies of
extraordinary merit.

" Bullet Proof."—Is the property of Mr. H. N. T. Jenner,
of Ranelagh Villas, Hove. He is by " Don Perseus," by " Don
Salano," ex " Andromeda," his dam, " Breach of Promise," being
by champion " Boaz," ex " Mods." Thus he is inbred to " Don
Pedro," and contains the valuable blood of " King Cole,"
champion " British Monarch," champion " His Lordship," and
champion " Ruling Passion." He is a dark brindle-pied,
weighing forty-eight pounds, active, vigorous, and healthy, with
well-shaped body, plenty of bone, good lay-back, deep stop, small
perfectly carried ears, and typical Bulldog expression. He has
sired some puppies of great promise, several of them having
already commenced a winning career.

" Uxbridge Morgan."—Is a white dog, possessing a body of unusual excellence, great width of front, short and compact, well-ribbed up, and with good bone. His finish of face, turn-up of underjaw, and Bulldog expression are capital. His sire "Hermit," was also sire of the celebrated champion "Heath Baronet," recently sold for £1,000, his dam, "Heath Baroness," being by "Heath Baron," ex "Passion." He is the property of Mr. W. R. Goodwin, of Spring Cottage, Oxted, Surrey, and of Kearney, Ontario, Canada. "Uxbridge Morgan" has won sixteen prizes, including five firsts and three seconds at the following shows :—Bulldog Club, Sandy, Ealing, New Cross, Waltham Cross, London Bulldog Society, and Brighton.

"**Miss Aubrey**," also the property of Mr. Goodwin, is a light-weight bitch of good quality. She is shapely in body, has large and well-formed skull, and possesses the right sort of Bulldog expression. She is by "Swashbuckler," ex "Leucha," he by champion "Bromley Crib," ex "Fifi," she by "Don Boaz," ex "Miss Persimmon."

"**Spa Victoria**" and "**Spa Country Girl.**"—The property of Mr. W. J. Plum, High Street, St. Neots, Hunts. "Spa Victoria" is a brindle, forty-two pounds weight, by "Uxbridge Matador," ex "Bonny Queen," he by "Salano Boy," ex "Northern Lady," by "Stormfiend," she by "Camberwell Crib," ex "Brompton Puss." She has a grand skull, short face, small rose ears, good cushion and furrow, well turned-up and wide underjaw, well-sprung ribs, and short tail. Winner of numerous prizes in strong competition at Kettering, Southwell, Bedford, Luton, Hitchin, Clerkenwell, Baldock, Sandy, under Messrs. Chaundler, Richards, Gresham, Madden, Taylor, Richardson. "Spa Country Girl," the daughter of the foregoing, was sired by "Probang" by champion "Prince Albert." She is white, with brindle markings, a light-weight of about thirty-two pounds. She is massive, thick-set, low to ground, very wide-fronted, good skull, ears (carried a trifle high), grand body and well-sprung ribs, very short crank tail, etc. Winner of numerous prizes, including ten guinea challenge cup, silver medals, special, first, second, and third prizes at Kettering, Nottingham, Southwell, Reading, Baldock, Sandy, Skegness, High Wycombe, Ealing, and Wallingford, under Messrs. Chaundler, Crocker, Richards, Holgate, Gresham, Cooper, Layton, Pegg, and Taylor.

"**Wilsid.**"—The property of Mr. W. P. Kidd, of Briar Cottage, Swinton, Manchester, is by champion "Prince Albert," ex "Sheba," by "President Carnot," ex "Ashton Mischief." She is thus "King Orry" bred on both sire and dam sides, which

"YOUNG SCORPION."

The property of
GEO. MURRELL, ESQ.,
PARAGON PLACE, BLACKHEATH,
LONDON, S.E.

Photo by H. St. John Cooper.

possibly accounts for the excellence of her type, character, and expression. " Wilsid " is a light brindle, weighs about forty-five pounds, is now thirteen months of age, having been born November 7th, 1903. Only exhibited on four occasions, viz., London Bulldog Club Show, Manchester Bulldog Club Show, Bradford, and Altrincham, she has won over twenty firsts, seconds, and specials. Never been beaten in puppy classes. She is a heavy-boned bitch, being no less than ten inches round her forearm to-day, has good shoulders, very short body, grand ribs, and well cut up in loin. In fact, Mr. Crabtree considers her the nearest to her sire in bitches ever bred. Her lay-back is exceptional, ears perfect, and some of our best judges say she has a bright future in store.

" **Hieland Dame,**" the property of Lieut. B. H. Baird, of Woodleigh, Cheltenham, by " What Ho Bob," ex " Klondike Nugget," he by Champion " Bromley Crib," ex " Lady Arundel," she by " Klondike," ex " Mr. Peek's Children." " Hieland Dame" has won forty first and special prizes in six months of this year (1904), including the Bulldog Club Novice Bowl, the Berrie Cup, the B.D.C. silver medal for the best bitch in the show at Bingley, and also numerous other specials, including a special for the best bitch of any variety in the show at Hunslet, and special for the best Bulldog or bitch. She is very typical of the Bromley Crib strain, and is full of " Prisoner " blood as well. She has a beautifully shaped body and really marvellous turn-up, with good square skull and right expression. She is thoroughly sound, and active as a kitten.

" **Totora.**"—The property of her breeder, Mr. C. J. Bridgland, of 70, High Road, Balham. " Totora " is by Mr. Pegg's well-known " Woodcote Galtee More," ex the winning bitch, " Princess Toto." She commenced her winning career when only seven months old at Wandsworth, where she won third novice, second puppy, and special in very strong competition. During the year 1904 she has been exhibited at Reigate, Lewes, Cruft's, Carshalton, Hastings, B.D.C. Show, Guildford, Nottingham, Eastbourne, Botanical Gardens, Redhill, and several other shows, winning over 140 firsts, cups, specials, and other prizes, including the British Bulldog Club's twenty-five guinea Challenge Cup, the Smartt's Punch Cup, twice Rodney Stone Cup, twice B.D.C. Novice Bowl, Nailsworth Cup, B.D.C. breeders' medal seven times, and silver medal four times. She is a dark brindle, with a well-chiselled head and most shapely body. She may be decidedly regarded as one of the best of living bitches, and still further improvement may be looked for in her, as she has plenty of time yet before her.

Champion "Rodney Smasher" is one of the only three America-bred champion Bulldogs, all of which were bred by Mr. C. G. Hopton, of Newark, New Jersey, U.S.A. "Smasher" is a brindle-pied, resembling in character his sire, champion "Rodney Rosador," who will be better remembered by English show-goers as "Nat Langham." At seven months old he won several firsts at the great New York Show, the puppy bowl and cup, and with "Rodney Myra" the Deal trophy, value £100, outright. Since then champion "Rodney Smasher" has pursued a winning career all over the American and Canadian continent, winning nearly 600 firsts and special prizes. He is extremely active, and, to demonstrate this, Mr. Hopton entered him in the half-mile walking handicap at Long Branch Show, which he won from scratch in a field of twelve in three minutes fifty-eight seconds. He is by champion "Rodney Rosador," ex "Rodney Caprice," she by "Bombard," by the celebrated champion "Boomerang." He was born in July, 1902, and weighs forty-two pounds.

"Lord Burley." This dog is the winner of very many prizes at all the best shows throughout the country, and is the property of an old-time breeder and fancier, Mr. George Murrell, of Paragon Place, Blackheath. He is by "Uxbridge Matador," by "Salano Boy," ex "Northern Queen," his dam, "Phillistine," being by champion "Rodney Stone," ex "Regent Street Princess." In body he is as near perfection as possible, having huge shoulders well set on, big rib, and fine loin, giving to it the right pear shape. His skull is massive, long and deep in face. He has plenty of bone and substance all through, and is a vigorous, strong, muscular dog of the right type. Among his winnings are two firsts, K.C. Show, 1902; two firsts, K.C. Show, 1903; first at L.K.A. Show, 1904, Wimbledon Canine Show, 1903; three firsts, Croydon, 1904; two firsts, Kensington; two seconds, Bulldog Club Show; three firsts, Bristol, 1903; two firsts, Manchester, 1903; two firsts, Birmingham, 1903; two firsts, Manchester, 1904; four firsts, King's Lynn, and cup for the best non-sporting dog or bitch in the show; and other prizes too numerous to mention. As a sire he is scarcely second to any in the kingdom. Some particularly fine puppies by him are shortly to make their debut. The photograph of him which appears in these pages cannot be regarded altogether as a satisfactory one, as it fails to do justice to his magnificent shoulders and great front. Heavy and massive though he is,

H

"LORD BURLEY."

The property of
GEORGE MURRELL, ESQ.,
PARAGON PLACE,
BLACKHEATH, S.E.

Photo by H. St. John Cooper.

he is an extremely active, not to say restless, dog, and the task of photographing him is not an enviable one. He is decidedly one of the very best dogs now appearing on the show bench, and, being as yet but little more than a puppy, has, no doubt, a great career before him.

"Young Scorpion," which is also the property of Mr. George R. Murrell, is a young brindle dog of unusual quality. He possesses in a marked degree all those points which are necessary for the making of a good dog. His bone is enormous, his skull big and flat. He has a rare turn-up of underjaw, with good lay-back and expression. In colour he is light brindle. He is a double cross of "Katapult," who was the sire of champion "Prince Albert." He weighs about fifty-two pounds, and, at the time of writing, is scarcely out of his puppyhood, as he was born only in August, 1903. When fully matured, he is a dog that will take his place with the best, as he possesses that quality, combined with substance, that must assuredly command success.

Champion "Regal Stone."—The property of Mr. W. Buckler, of Brookfield, West Hill, Highgate, London, N. A son of Mr. Walter Jefferies' late champion "Rodney Stone," and possessing to the full all those points and characteristics that have made the "Stone" strain of Bulldogs famous the world over. "Regal Stone" has proved himself to be a worthy son of his sire, and of his dam, "Lady Patricia." He is a brindle dog with a phenomenal skull, massive and correct in shape, heavily wrinkled, with a good competent nose well set back, and an underjaw that is all that a Bulldog's underjaw should be, short bodied, of great width in front, and finely made in the rear; he is the possessor of immense bone, and is thoroughly typical in all respects. He is the winner of a great number of prizes, all won in the strongest competition, and as he is exhibited by his owner only at the most important shows in the country, where all the pick of Bulldogdom is exhibited, his winnings thus place him in the very front rank of living Bulldogs. At the 1903 show of the Bulldog Club Incorporated he won five first prizes and the Championship, beating all the best dogs of the day, including "Heath Baronet." At the Kennel Club Show in the same year he won in the open and limit classes, again beating the best dogs in the country. Here he took reserve for the Championship, though the winner of this honour might not only have given place to "Regal Stone," but to perhaps half a dozen other dogs as well, such dogs for instance as champions "Felton Prince," "Heath Baronet," and "Nuthurst Doctor," everyone of which has proved himself a better dog than the Championship winner on this occasion. At

Bristol, 1903, he was again the winner of several firsts, in strong competition, and again beat "Heath Baronet," whom he has defeated nine times, and this time was reserved for the Championship, which was gained by that notable little dog, "Prince Albert;" second at Cruft's, 1904, he in the same month won two firsts at Cheltenham, beating the winning dog at Cruft's, and securing his second Championship. He was second at Manchester, 1904, to champion "Broadlea Squire," and at Birmingham in the same year won first and Championship, thus qualifying himself for the title of "Champion."

"**Ingoldsby Lawyer.**"—The property of H. St. John Cooper, of Oxberry, Surrenden Road, Brighton. A massive heavy-weight, weighing sixty pounds, excelling in Bulldog type, character, and expression, and possessing a wonderful skull, big nose, and great bone throughout. Had this dog been shorter in back he would have been in the very front rank, as it is, he is winner of firsts at Brighton, 1903, Lewes, Eastbourne, Hastings, and Brighton, 1904, and winner twice in succession of the South Coast Kennel Society's Challenge Bowl, for the best dog of any breed in the show, at the Club's open shows in 1903 and 1904, beside numerous other specials. "Ingoldsby Lawyer" was born December 24th, 1897, and died while this book was in the press, December 26th, 1904.

"**Mersham Jingo.**"—The property of his breeder, Mrs. Carlo Clarke, Radnage Farm, Stokenchurch, Bucks. "Mersham Jingo" is a low, cloddy, little brindle, exceptionally good in barrel, being short and compact, with big ribs, deep in brisket, and nicely cut-up in loin. His head will always bear the closest examination, skull being big in circumference, and long from ear to eye, with rare depth of face, and very large nostrils. For placement of shoulders and bone very few of our present Bulldogs can compare with this celebrated son of "Mersham Jumbo." "Mersham Jingo" made his début at Birkenhead, when only ten months old. He obtained the following honours in the strongest competition : first maiden, four entries; first novice, ten entries; first puppy and second to champion "Broadlea Squire" in limit, the judge being Mr. Hartley. Under Mr. Harding Cox, at Hastings, in 1903, he won first limit, first novice, and second puppy (beaten by that good bitch, "Lottie Lennox"). Mrs. Clarke refused £60 for him at the show. He then won at Bishop's Stortford, under Mr. Woodiwiss, third limit and first puppy, and at Richmond, under the same judge, second and third puppy. At the Ladies' Kennel Association, Botanic Gardens, 1903, he had a field-day under the Rev. Madden,

"DISMAL JIMMY."

The property of
MRS. CLAUDE PAYNE,
THE MANOR, SHILLINGTON,
HERTS.

winning first puppy, first novice, and first limit, and a host of specials. In 1904, £100 was offered by an American fancier. At the Bulldog Club Show in May, he won third breeders. Owing to his having distemper so badly, he was not used at stud till lately, and his first litter was born in March, 1904. Mrs. Clarke has two very promising dogs by him, and both have already won in puppy classes.—

His pedigree is as follows :—

			Mersham Jingo				
Mersham Jumbo.					Mersham Venus.		
Buck.		Pressmoor Flo.		Donax.		Mersham Goody Two Shoes.	
Ch. Bedgebury Lion.	Bedgebury Gipsy.	Don Salano.	Pressmore Pleasure.	Ch. Dockleaf.	Donna Disdain.	Buck.	Pressmore Flo

"Mersham Jumbo."—The property of Mrs. Carlo Clarke. This massive heavy-weight brindle, which was bred by his owner, proves in himself and his progeny the satisfactory result to be attained by careful and scientific breeding. He is one of the results of Mrs. Clarke's favourite breeding theories, the alliance of the blood of champion "Bedgebury Lion," with that of "Don Salano." Other notable successes achieved by Mrs. Clarke by a careful mixture of these two Bulldog strains are "Mersham Jock," now an American champion, and "Mersham Billy," who is in far away Australia. "Mersham Jumbo" has many prizes to his credit, he having won upwards of 250 during his show career. His bone is phenomenal, immense depth of brisket, yet despite his great size, he is the most active and nimble of dogs. He is the sire of some extraordinary good stock, including "Mersham Jingo." Among his bench successes are the Bulldog Society's Breeders' Gold Medal, the Bulldog Club's Puppy Bowl, five times (beating all records), the Berrie Cup, and twenty times winner of the Breeders' Bronze Medal for the best dog in show, bred by Exhibitor.

"Kilburn King."—The property of H. Schlaferman, Esq., 112, Goldhawk Road, Shepherd's Bush, London. "Kilburn King" is a tiger brindle, closely resembling his sire, the famous "Klondike," who is also the property of Mr. Schlaferman. A heavy-weight of fifty-five pounds, he is remarkable for his quality, and there is not the slightest inclination to that coarseness which is so usual with heavy-weight dogs. His skull and fore-face are worthy of all admiration. He is sound and active, with strong and massive bone, fine and well-carried ears, and a grand turn-up of underjaw. He has won at almost all the leading shows, and is siring puppies of very great promise, as may easily be supposed, taking his breeding into consideration.

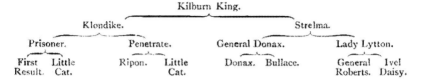

Kilburn King.			
Klondike.		Strelma.	
Prisoner.	Penetrate.	General Donax.	Lady Lytton.
First Result. Little Cat.	Ripon. Little Cat.	Donax. Bullace.	General Roberts. Ivel Daisy.

"**Kilburn President.**"—The property of Mr. Schlaferman. A very compact golden brindle, weighing forty-two pounds. He is a winner every time shewn. Like his kennel-mate, "Kilburn King," is a stock-getter of great value. He is a grandson of the celebrated champion "Boaz" (Mr. Schlaferman's), and combines the valuable "Wild Fang" blood with that of the brothers "Stockwell" and "Don Salano."

His pedigree is as follows :—

Kilburn President.			
Pentemenon.		Endion Queen.	
Champion Boaz.	Mods.	Ivan.	Cowley Tartlet
Stockwell.	Champion Lord Dora II. Blackberry. Nelson III.	Wild Tricks. Fang.	Don Cowley Salano. Belle.

"**Probang.**"—The property of Mrs. Claude Paine, Shillington, Herts. A son of that marvellous sire, champion "Prince Albert," ex "Sniffler." "Probang" is a massive heavy-weight white dog, a good big dog in every sense of the words. He possesses a grand skull, with typical head, good nose, ears, bone, and a shapely body, to which the illustration of him in this book scarcely does justice. He has done a great deal of winning at the best shows, and amongst trophies he has won are the British Bulldog Club's twenty-five guinea Challenge Cup, and the Bromley Crib Challenge Shield. He is a stock-getter of the first magnitude, and like his sire has the power of transmitting his qualities to his progeny.

"**Dismal Jimmy.**"—Bred and owned by Mrs. Claude Paine. A compact good-bodied dog, excelling in skull, wrinkle and finish of face, naturally wide fronted, with good depth of brisket, strong in underjaw, and good ears. He is a dog that has as yet been little shown, but has succeeded in winning some forty prizes at the best shows, including the Bulldog Club's Puppy and Novice Cups, and the British Bulldog Club's twenty-five guinea Challenge Cup ; others of his wins are, firsts at Sandy,

"PROBANG."

The property of
    MRS. CLAUDE PAYNE,
    THE MANOR, SHILLINGTON,
    HERTS.

the London Bulldog Society's Show, and the Kennel Club Show, 1904. He is by "Klondike," ex "Kilburn Prospect."

"**Bob Upanwyn.**"—The property of Mrs. Jemmett Browne, 50, Ashburnham Mansions, Chelsea, London. Whelped on June 27th, 1903. This dog is a dark brindle, excelling in head properties, capital length of skull, wrinkle, turn-up, lay-back, and bone. His body is cobby, well set up, short roach back, and neat little tail; he is a good mover, and a thoroughly sound dog in all respects. He has been shown very seldom, four times in all, but has rendered a good account of himself. He made his début at the age of eight months, at the British Bulldog Club Show at Manchester, where he won first and two seconds; at Stretford he won first puppy; at Altrincham under Mr. Deacon, first novice; and at Bristol first limit, first juniors, first novice, second breeders, and third open. Many experienced breeders consider that this dog has a great future before him. He is by "Clansman," ex "Girtford Grisette," by champion "Prince Albert," and was bred by his owner.

"**Andrew Praze.**"—Litter brother to above, owned and bred by Mrs. Jemmett Browne. This dog, a fawn, with tremendous length and breadth of skull, great bone, heavily wrinkled, well broken-up face, and short down tail, promises to fully equal his brother, "Bob Upanwyn," but is a later dog to make up. He has been shown only once, and that at the Wimbledon Canine Society's Open Show, where in a novice class of twenty-two he won third prize, he being then barely out of his puppyhood. He has plenty of Bulldog character, good expression, and, like his brother, is a thoroughly sound dog.

"**Ortersutem.**"—This fine, dark brindle bitch, bred by Mrs. Jemmett Browne, by "Dathan," ex "Wattlewyn," is the winner of over 200 prizes and specials, including reserve for Championship twice, the B.B.D.C. fifty guinea Challenge Cup, the Berrie Cup, all the Bulldog Club's Novice Cups, specials for best bitch in show at Hatfield. She possesses a most shapely body, splendid lay-back and underjaw, rare length of skull and spring of rib. She may certainly be regarded as one of the best bitches of the day. She has rare character and the proper Bulldog expression, with no suspicion of "softness."

"**Girtford Goody.**" by "Ivel Doctor," ex "Ivel Dorry," is probably the best-bodied bitch alive; in fact, it would be impossible to find fault with her body; while in skull and underjaw there is very little to be desired. A white bitch, with black brindle-marked head, she has won several prizes, including two seconds, Bulldog Club Show, 1903, first Streatham, second

Sandy, and the special for the best-bodied dog or bitch in the show. She is the property of Mrs. Jemmett Browne.

Champion " Broadlea Squire." This splendid Bulldog, the property of Mr. J. W. Proctor, was sired by Mr. Crabtree's champion " Prince Albert," whose best son he is without a doubt. Of this dog nothing can be said but what is good, and his excellence is proved by the immense number of prizes he has won under all the leading judges at the best shows in the country. He has won all the trophies of the three Bulldog Clubs. This dog has had a well-nigh unbroken series of successes, and may be rightly regarded as, if not the, at any rate one, of the very best Bulldogs in the country.

" Buddug," K.C.S.B. 860 F.—The property of Mrs. W. W. Crocker. This little red smut is generally regarded as being one of the best all-round bitches in the fancy. In her show career she has fully confirmed all her owner's expectations, and, indeed, has fully proved her right to the name she bears, " Buddug " being the Welsh for " Victorious." In nose, underjaw, shape, and type generally she is particularly strong, and as a good all-round specimen of the breed, she deserves to take rank with the best in the land. She is a brilliant example of the policy of breeding to a low, cloddy type, which is the correct one. At the same time, she is a refutation of the idea, which has almost passed into a proverb, that underjaw and face finish do not accompany the low, cloddy body, short back, and short legs of the ideal Bulldog. To a long list of previous wins, including victories at Cruft's and Manchester, she has during the last season (1904) added the following victories to her already plethoric list :—First and Championship, Cheltenham ; first, open, and four specials, Streatham ; first, open, B.B. Club fifty guinea Challenge Cup, Berrie Cup, etc., Sandy ; first, open, and Berrie Cup, Chelmsford, under Mr. G. W. Richards ; first, open, Championship, B.B. Club fifty guinea Challenge Cup, Berrie Cup, etc., Bristol, under Mr. E. H. Bowers ; second, open, Richmond, under Mr. R. D. Thomas ; second, open, and six specials, Botanic Gardens, under Mr. Mackness ; third, open, Crystal Palace, under Mr. L. Crabtree. Her weight, in show form, is now thirty-six pounds. She is by " Merlin," and her dam " Sinfi Lovell," also bred by Mrs. Crocker, who is justly proud of having bred this good specimen.

" Lord Milner."—The property of Mrs. W. H. Ford, Harrow, Middlesex. This fine young brindle dog has had a most successful show career, having won some hundred or more first prizes and specials, and the Championship at the Incorporated

"LORD MILNER."

The property of
       MRS. W. H. FORD,
       STATION ROAD,
       HARROW, MIDDLESEX.

Club's Show, 1904, at the Crystal Palace. He has a great skull, with extraordinary finish of face, and broad, upturned underjaw, big nose, and eyes very wide apart. He is low to ground, with great depth of brisket and fine spring of rib, while his limbs are well formed and very strong in bone. He is by the well-known "Klondike" by "Prisoner" ex "Penetrate," his dam, "Lady Lottie," being by "Pentemenon" by champion "Boaz" ex "Cornflower," by "General Roberts."

Without a reference to the dogs of that most successful of breeders, Mr. Walter Jefferies, of Roseneath Grove Park, Denmark Hill, London, this chapter would indeed be like the play of *Hamlet* minus the character of the Prince of Denmark. Mr. Jefferies made his first step towards Bulldog fame by breeding that grand champion, "Rodney Stone," which was afterwards bought by Mr. Croker for the then record and sensational price of a thousand pounds. Splendid though the sum, Mr. Jefferies in reality gained far more than that by mating his bitch "Lucy Loo" with Mr. R. G. S. Mann's "John o' the Funnels," for "Rodney Stone," the result of that union, has founded for Mr. Jefferies a strain of Bulldogs that must make, and, indeed, already has made, its influence felt in the Bulldog world, and which will be very prominent indeed in the history of the Bulldog that is to come. Many—and here the writer will confess that he was of the number—were inclined to regard the production of "Rodney Stone" as a lucky fluke, for which Mr. Jefferies was rather to be envied than admired. But the subsequent history of the Roseneath Kennels and the Stone strain must convince all fair-minded people that Mr. Jefferies is possessed of a knowledge of the science of breeding that is as unusual as it has been in his case consistently successful. Champion "Rodney Stone" possessed to the full the power of transmitting his superlative qualities to his offspring, and it seems that the gift is hereditary, for the "Stone" Bulldogs, while bearing a strong family resemblance to each other and to the founder of their strain, are slowly but surely improving with each generation; and Mr. Jefferies, recognising that "Rodney Stone," good though he was, had yet his faults, has, by judicious selection and mating, been steadily working towards that goal which is the ambition of every earnest breeder—"the perfect dog." Whether he has already succeeded or no remains yet to be proved, but of "Dick Stone," a youngster now in the Roseneath Kennels, it has been written, "'Dick Stone' is the best Bulldog ever bred." He is a red-pied heavy-weight, inbred to "Rodney Stone," for he is by "British Stone" (himself a dog of extraordinary merit, but

debarred from the show bench by reason of a maimed foot) ex a
" Rodney Stone " bred bitch. Besides this dog, the Roseneath
kennels possesses " British Stone," his sire, " Buckstone," by
" Rodney Stone," ex " Black 'Un," a grand brindle that has sired
many winners ; " Royal Stone," for whom a sum almost as
large as that paid for " Rodney Stone " has been refused, and
" Rex Stone," brother to Mr. Buckler's champion " Regal Stone,"
and himself, did Mr. Jefferies care to exhibit him, easily the
winner of many a championship, as indeed would be at least four
out of these five remarkable dogs.

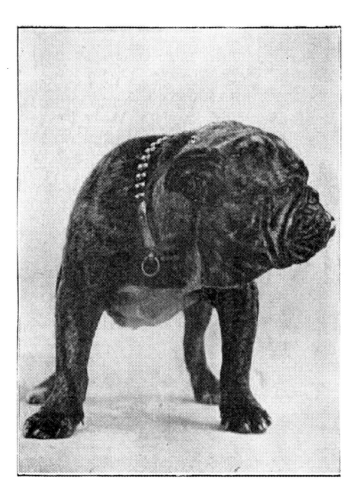

"PRINCE OF DARKNESS."

The property of
     MRS. MAY,
     " SANDHURST,"
     MARINE DRIVE, RHYL.

CHAPTER IX.

CONCLUSION.

It was confidently believed and stated, many years ago, that when Bull-baiting became illegal, the race of dogs that had been bred especially for that sport would speedily become extinct. Those who made this statement have proved to be false prophets ; and it would no doubt greatly surprise them, and, perhaps, also mystify them, could it be possible for them to witness the present and ever-growing popularity of the English Bulldog.

While there are thousands who keep, breed, and exhibit Bull-dogs, there are many thousands more who would start Bulldog kennels were they not deterred by the greatly-exaggerated stories that one is constantly hearing of the Bulldog's delicate constitution, his restricted powers of locomotion, and his uselessness as a guard of persons and property. Unfortunately, there is some truth in the statement that he is a delicately constituted dog. During puppyhood he is perhaps, especially prone to puppy ailments, and no doubt requires more care and attention than do puppies of other and hardier breeds. But puppyhood once passed, the properly reared Bulldog is no weakling, and should give his owner but little trouble and anxiety.

Codling is never to be recommended ; and from the day of his birth the animal should be obliged to lead as hardy and as healthy a life as circumstances will permit. He should not live in an artificially heated kennel, and treated indeed as one would treat a hot-house plant; and it must always be remembered that it is quite possible to kill a dog by kindness of a mistaken nature, and that, in fact, in the case of valuable puppies, more are killed by kindness than by neglect.

Over-feeding and artificial heating should be carefully guarded against ; both defeat their own object. Exercise is of the first necessity ; and if dogs were properly exercised from their earliest days we should hear far less of and see fewer cripples. Kept

The American Champion—"RODNEY SMASHER."

The property of
    C. J. HOPTON, ESQ.,
    NEWARK, N.J., U.S.A.

free from worms, properly fed, properly housed and exercised, and last, but by no means less in importance, groomed vigorously every day with a dandy brush, to keep his coat clean and his skin healthy, there is no reason why a puppy, bred from good, healthy, and sound stock, should not reach maturity, and in his or her turn beget more sound and healthy stock, which should cause the breeder and owner very little more trouble than he would experience with admittedly hardier breeds of dogs.

There is no royal road to Bulldog breeding ; but the man who is possessed of a large share of common sense, and who is willing to apply it to the subject, who is resolved that his dogs shall live healthy lives, eat health-giving food, and have their full share of health-giving exercise, and who, above all, can make his start with a good share of enthusiasm, and an inborn love of the dog, need have no fears. Disappointments he will assuredly meet with, but they will make his successes all the more prized ; for success that is easily attained is never valued like that which has been achieved after strenuous efforts, and after disappointments patiently borne with.

THE END.

AT STUD NEAR LONDON.

BOB UPANWYN

Clansman   Girtford Grisette

Rex Nelson   Donax Baby   Ch. Prince Albert   Moston Busy

(See Coloured Plate and description in Chapter on Prominent Dogs
of the Day.)

Fee, £5 5s.

ANDREW PRAZE,

Litter brother to above.   Fawn.   *(See Illustration and description in Book.)*

Fee, £3 3s.

WILL MAYKANAYME,

Litter brother to above.   A compact, cobby, light-weight dog, great
width of skull, good body, short down tail, small rose ears, low to ground,
and great bone—a real typical bulldog.   He has been only twice shown,
winning 2nd Puppy, and 10 Guinea Challenge Cup.

Fee, £2 2s.

Apply, **C. JEMMETT BROWNE, East Common, Harpenden, Herts. ; or
50, Ashburnham Mansions, Chelsea.**

GEORGE ROBERT MURRELL,

THE KENNELS,

PARAGON PLACE, BLACKHEATH, LONDON, S.E., England,

HAS owned some of the very best Bulldogs that have ever lived, such as Champions Prince Albert,* King Lud,‡ Duke of Albemarle, King Orry,‡ Lottie Lenox, Colenso,‡ Sheriff,‡ General French,‡ Hucknall Gipsy,‡ Chibob,‡ also such noted dogs sprung from his kennels as Champions Boomerang, Katafelto, Broadlea Squire, etc., etc.,

Offers at Stud the following grandly bred Dogs, rich in the bloods of above-mentioned Dogs :—

No. 1. LORD BURLEY.

Born May 21st, 1902, weight about 50 lbs. This dog, as must be expected, has huge shoulders and a big rib, and fine loin (rarely seen now), big long skull, deep in face, eyes, ears, and tail perfect, with plenty of bone and substance. A vigorous, strong, muscular dog (not soft and fat), a sure stock-getter. The challenge still stands good to match two pups by him against any two of a litter. Nearly his first get. Fee at present, **£4 4s.** *See illustration.*

No. 2. YOUNG SCORPION.

This dog has a double cross of G.R.M.'s late Katapult in him—Katapult the sire of Champion Prince Albert. He is one of the finest young dogs ever seen. Whelped August 10th, 1903, weight about 52 lbs. *See illustration.* Fee at present, **£3 3s.**

No. 3. The Noted Dog, KENTISH DUKE.

Own brother to Kentish Belle and Floradora. See "Dogs of the 19th Century." Kentish Duke is sire of the much-talked-of Orry Model*‡ and Chesterton,* both bred by G.R.M. Fee at present, **£3 3s.** Kentish Duke has the grandest head of any Bulldog living.

No. 4. STORMLIGHT.

Weight 50 lbs., rich fawn, and a rare bred one, being by Scorpion by Woodcote Galtee More ex. Miss Bombard by Bombard, and out of own sister to Kentish Duke, a double cross again of Katapult. Fee, **£3 3s.**

No. 5. A small brindle pied dog by Swashbuckler ex. the prize bitch Leucha, and own brother to the prize bitch, Miss Aubrey. Fee, **£2 2s.**

All the above dogs are of the highest breed and most carefully bred for strength of character, pluck, big, strong top and bottom jaws, none of your retiring, nervous sort with weak underjaws and rickety (both go together), but dogs able to uphold their name, and stock-getters. Several young dogs, both sexes ; also puppies at reasonable prices.

Dogs marked * bred by G. R. MURRELL, and those marked ‡ are a few of very many exported to the United States of America. G.R.M. has the very highest testimonials from some of the leading breeders and exhibitors of America, Continent, etc.

NOTE ADDRESS.

THE MERSHAM

TEAM of STUD BULLDOGS

FOR

TOY BREEDING.

Mersham Gilfain, by Sir Jasper Thorndyke, ex. Tremula, brindle white, weight 28 lbs., litter brother to the sensational Stokenchurch Dolores; pure rose ears, and of English type, but gets very small puppies.   **Fee, £3 3s.**

Mersham Planet, weight 23½ lbs. Golden brindle, by King of Thanet, ex. Mona, thus pure English blood. Has marvellous under-jaw, turn-up and lay-back.   **Fee, £3 3s.**

Mersham Jum Jum, dark brindle, by Woodcote Tom Thumb, ex. Brunette (weight 15 lbs.), weight 30 lbs. A wonderfully cloddy short backed dog with rose ears.   **Fee, £3 3s.**

Mersham Tiny Tee To Tum, by Polo et. Bagatelle ex. Amelia Maude, weight 21 lbs.; pure French type but with rose ears. This is a very cloddy little dog, with wonderful bone, and has won whenever shown.   **Fee, £4 4s.**

Tweedledee, dark brindle, by Ch. Pere Boojum, ex. Cora, weight 24 lbs. Has lovely rose ears, and is a very compact, active little dog.   **Fee, £2 2s.**

For Stud Cards, etc., apply

W. WOODHOUSE, Kennelman,

RADNAGE FARM HOUSE, STOKENCHURCH, Bucks.

Station—West Wycombe, G.W.R.

THE MERSHAM BULLDOGS AT STUD

THE PROPERTY OF MRS. CARLO F. C. CLARKE.

"MERSHAM BANG."

MERSHAM JUMBO
(SEE ILLUSTRATION).

MERSHAM JINGO
(SEE ILLUSTRATION).

MERSHAM DANDY.

MERSHAM MARVEL.

MERSHAM BANG.

Stud Cards and all Particulars from Head Kennelman, W. WOODHOUSE.

RADNAGE FARM, STOKENCHURCH, BUCKS.

AYLESBURY
HOUND MEAL,

SUITABLE FOR ALL BREEDS OF DOGS.

This Meal is not composed of Broken Biscuits, but is a complete change from all other Makers' Meals.

Mr. G. W. RICHARDS writes us on 8/4/04 :—

"GREENLANDS," HEVER, KENT.

GENTLEMEN,

I was quite out of Hound Meal when yours arrived yesterday, and had been obliged to get some ordinary Dog Biscuits for my Bulldogs, but after being fed for so long a time on your Meal, they all refused to eat the other kind of biscuits. This, I think, is a pretty good sign they know what is best for them.

The above testimonial is one from many that we have received.

Price, 15/- per cwt. ; 8/- ½ cwt.
Carriage Paid for Cash with Order.

For Samples and further particulars, write

THE SOLE MANUFACTURERS,
The Aylesbury Foods Co., Ltd.,
AYLESBURY.

"FLAKO" COOKED FOOD for DOGS.

Photo.] **WE ALL LIKE "FLAKO"** *[H. St. John Cooper, Esq*

MERSHAM JINGO. MERSHAM BANG. MERSHAM MARVEL.

The Property of (MRS.) C. F. C. CLARKE.

HIGHLY NUTRITIOUS. VERY DIGESTIBLE. MOST ECONOMICAL.

13/5 per 112 lbs. **7/=** per 56 lbs.

Samples Free. *Carriage Paid.* *Cash with Order.*

To be obtained from Corn Dealers, and the Army and Navy Auxiliary Supply, Ltd.

SOLE MAKERS:

UVECO CEREALS, Ltd., Wallasey Mills, BIRKENHEAD

FOR KEEPING DOGS

IN GOOD HEALTH & CONDITION USE

"CARTA CARNA" Dog Foods

No. 1, for Large Dogs; No. 2, Terrier food; No. 3, Puppy food; No. 4, for Toy

AND AS A CHANGE,

"CHAMPION" Dog Biscuits.

Illustrated CATALOGUE and Samples Free.

SOLE MANUFACTURERS:

F. C. LOWE & SON

Limited,

"Carta Carna" Works, Sittingbourne, Kent.

CPSIA information can be obtained at www.ICGtesting.com
Printed in the USA
LVOW091924190312

273837LV00003B/4/A